What Is Living, What Is Dead in Christianity Today?

What Is Living, What Is Dead in Christianity Today?

Breaking the Liberal-Conservative Deadlock

Charles Davis

Harper & Row, Publishers, San Francisco

Cambridge, Hagerstown, New York, Philadelphia, Washington
London, Mexico City, São Paulo, Singapore, Sydney

For information address Harper & Row, Publishers, Inc., 10 East 53rd Street, New York, NY 10022. Published simultaneously in Canada by Fitzhenry & Whiteside, Limited, Toronto.

FIRST EDITION

Library of Congress Cataloging-in-Publication Data

Davis, Charles, 1923–
What is living, what is dead in Christianity today?

1. Christianity—Essence, genius, nature. I. Title.
BR121.2.D32 1986 201 85-51556
ISBN 0-86683-511-3

86 87 88 89 90 RRD 10 9 8 7 6 5 4 3 2 1

FOR CLAIRE

Whose growth has been for me
  a sign that,
          "nature is never spent;
There lives the dearest freshness deep down things."

Gerard Manley Hopkins

Yet not too like, yet not so like to be
Too near, too clear, saving a little to endow
Our feigning with the strange unlike, whence
springs
The difference that heavenly pity brings.

Wallace Stevens

In the present connection, *reconstruction* signifies taking a theory apart and putting it back together again in a new form in order to attain more fully the goal it has set for itself.

Jürgen Habermas

Contents

Acknowledgment

This book is the fruit of a Killam Research Fellowship, granted by the Canada Council for 1981–3. I have to thank the Killam Trustees and the Canada Council for the exceptional and enriching experience of two years of uninterrupted reflection and research.

Charles Davis

Introduction

The reflections in this book had their starting point in the last chapter of my previous book, *Theology and Political Society*.[1] There I distinguished the "private self" of bourgeois individualism from the "interior self" of all genuine religious faith. The "interior self" I identified with the mystical element of religion; I saw it as releasing human persons into individual freedom as subjects. Though apolitical in the sense of transcending any and every political order, the mystical element was eminently political as grounding politics as a process of communication among fully individual subjects in freedom. Without a transcendent grounding, politics deteriorates into mere administration, and the individual faces abolition as an archaic survival in an increasingly bureaucratized social system.

The "interior self" differs from the "private self" in not being confined to the private sphere. The stress upon the transcendent and indefeasibly individual core of the human subject is not a Romantic flight from politics and social concern. The "interior self" is mediated socially, attaining its identity only in and through a tradition. Likewise, it finds expression only in the context of a tradition, so that the outlet for its original contribution as an individual is a transformative critique of the tradition within which it arises as a self. The question, however, is what kind of social mediation, social expression, social concern, and social practice is appropriate for the "interior self" thus defined.

In the last chapter of *Theology and Political Society* I moved decisively away from what I still consider the parochial exclusiveness of most Christian theologians, whether Catholic or Protestant, including the representatives of political theology and the theologies of liberation, towards the openness to other religious traditions as found in Wilfred Cantwell Smith.[2] As Smith eloquently argues in his many books, the religious history of humankind is in plain historical fact a unity, insofar as the history of each religious tradition is intertwined with the history of the rest, so that the history of any one tradition is a strand in a more complex whole. Further, as Smith also argues, what is happening is the convergence of the various traditions, not towards a flat, homogeneous unity of all religions, but towards the formation of a variegated, critical, global self-consciousness in which we come together in communication and partnership, acknowledging the unity that binds us together despite the persistent plurality of our traditions.

I am not so sure as Smith is that the corporate, global self-consciousness now struggling to be born will find adequate expression through adapting the existing religious traditions. It is possible that the pluralistic approach marks their desuetude and the movement towards new forms of expressing the transcendent dimension of human life. No doubt there will be continuity as well as discontinuity, but how far present identities and distinctions will be preserved is difficult to determine. My concern here is, however, the more limited one of determining the social practice adequate to the "interior self" of Christian faith. This cannot be limited to a Christian context. It cannot be defined simply as the translation into concrete reality of the demands of the Christian gospel. What it requires is the collaboration among people from various traditions in the formation of a universal social order, which as universal will not be distinctively and exclusively Christian. In other words, there is no way in which we can make one religious tradition, our own, the universal horizon, the exclusive basis for a universal order. Yet such a universal social order is a requirement not just for the *bene esse,* but for the *esse* or very survival of humankind. There is a sense indeed in which every religious tradition establishes a universal horizon, since as religious it is concerned with ultimates. Nevertheless there are various patterns of symbolic expressions of those ultimates, and their variety constitutes the variety of religious traditions. Despite unresolvable contradictions, a complementarity binds the religious traditions together and allows them to collaborate in confronting present social, cultural, and political problems. These cannot be met from the standpoint of an exclusive claim to universality on the part of any one tradition. The failure to recognize that renders much Christian theology today myopic and provincial.

The originality of political theology and of the theologies of liberation lies not in their content but in their formal structure. In their content for the most part they repeat and reappropriate traditional, though frequently neglected, themes. Where they are original is in their insistence that social and political action enters intrinsically into the hermeneutic process, so that the interpretation of the Christian tradition is mediated through actual social and political reality. But what has not been clearly seen is that such mediation has to become a critical, dialectical mediation if one is to avoid distorting the tradition into an ideological reflection of one or other of protagonist groups in the existing situation. This means that the tradition is involved in a constant process of deconstruction and reconstruction as the implications of its own praxis in ever-new situations transforms its theoretical self-understanding. The dialectical process should not be confused with a compromising adaptation to fashionable attitudes. It represents the dynamic of the tradition itself in its life-situation. Compromise that betrays the tradition results from attempts to keep an earlier form of the tradition intact in new conditions conceived as only externally related to it.

What I was pointing to in my remarks on pluralism and new religious identity in *Theology and Political Society* was that the living out of the present situation was breaking apart Christian exclusiveness and transforming the Christian tradition so as to open it to the complementary insights and affirmations of the other major religious traditions. The present social, cultural, and political demands cannot be met from within an exclusively Christian horizon or from the resources of the Christian tradition alone. That Latin American liberation theology confines itself to the elaboration of Christian ideas and themes, fertilized by some Marxist elements, is understandable because of the persistence of a mutual involvement of the Christian Church and society in that region, though the sharing of Latin America in the general problems of the Third World should provoke a wider perspective. But it is less excusable that European political theology, with its American followers, should still consider it possible to do theology on the assumption that the Christian tradition in an exclusive fashion represented the definitive truth concerning human life and destiny. It may be partly the academic setting of much theology, making theologians unwilling to venture beyond their area of acknowledged competence to speak of other religions and cultures, that leaves theologians writing as though they could meet the present world situation by further refining traditional concepts on the person and work of Jesus Christ. The relationship with Judaism alone, not to mention other traditions, and the imperative, now widely recognized, of not delegitimizing the Jewish religion by the form and content of the Christian claim for Christ indicate plainly enough that one cannot continue to suppose that the Christian religion in its inherited form has some exclusive and final answer to the problems of humankind. It is one element in a complex whole, subject to a dialectical development in a movement towards a world order of a yet unforeseen composition.

The mention of the relationship between Christianity and Judaism puts me in mind of the work of Rosemary Ruether,[3] and this in turn leads me to acknowledge the bold character of feminist theology as compared with the clinging to received habits of thought characteristic of male academic theology. In writing of literary criticism, the English Marxist critic Terry Eagleton, after outlining the features of a revolutionary literary criticism, continues:

> If one wanted a paradigm for such criticism, already established within the present, there is a name for it: feminist criticism. No other form of criticism over the past decade has fought so fiercely and consistently to unite all of these objectives. While Marxist criticism has been largely enshrined within the academy, feminist criticism, though often actually produced there, transgresses those boundaries and takes its primary impulse from a political movement.[4]

Admittedly, Eagleton immediately qualifies his remarks with some serious reservations about actual achievement of feminist criticism as distinct from promise. Nevertheless, his main assessment as quoted can be, I think, transferred to feminist theology. There, unlike elsewhere, we experience a decisive break with the conformism of received theology, whatever may be the limitations of present achievement.

Eagleton's analysis of a revolutionary literary criticism may be used—no doubt beyond his own intention and desire—to give a clue as to what would be a critical theology. He writes:

> It [revolutionary literary criticism] would dismantle the ruling concepts of "literature", reinserting "literary" texts into the whole field of cultural practices. It would strive to relate such "cultural" practices to other forms of social activity, and to transform the cultural apparatuses themselves. It would articulate its "cultural" analyses with a consistent political intervention. It would deconstruct the received hierarchies of "literature" and transvaluate received judgments and assumptions; engage with the language and "unconscious" of literary texts, to reveal their role in the ideological construction of the subject; and mobilize such texts, if necessary by hermeneutic "violence" in a struggle to transform those subjects within a wider political context.[5]

While as basically a liberal I have my hesitations about the pretensions implicit in the designation "revolutionary," I do think that this passage can serve to indicate how a critical theology can relate itself to an emancipatory practice. It must dismantle the ruling concepts of religion, reinserting religious texts into the whole field of cultural practices. It should articulate its cultural analyses with a consistent political intervention. It must engage with the language and the unconscious of religious texts, to reveal their role in the ideological construction of the subject. The texts are to be mobilized beyond straightforward and received interpretations for a transformation of the subject within a wider political context.

Before I wrote this book, the project I had in mind was the development of a critical theology which on the basis of a critical theory of society and history would elaborate a fresh hermeneutic of Christian beliefs and texts. I found myself, however, engaged as in a prolegomenon to that task, trying to order and make sense of the variety of symbol systems that had characterized the Christian religion in the course of its history and still marked it today. Since there would seem to be an affinity between the choice of a symbol system and social and political attitudes, the elaboration of typology of Christian symbol systems came within the scope of a political theology and went beyond the limits of a mere prolegomenon. Nevertheless I recognize how much is still to be done before one can speak of a critical theology in more than a pretentious way.

A word may be added here about the social and political implications of symbolism and figurative language. Our society is caught today in a swing between metaphysics and nihilism. Metaphysics attempts to come to terms with the temporal flux of appearances by positing unchanging archetypes or essences or some form of invariant principles of knowledge or of being. The swing away from metaphysics is not simply the loss of an abstract belief in heavenly essences but a repulsion from the social and political implications of such belief. Metaphysics is linked to oppressive social structures and authoritarian political regimes. Appeal to unchanging essences or principles is used to block any change in the established order and to crush any protest against heteronomous power structures. Nihilism, on its part, does not necessarily leave the chaos of the temporal flux untouched. The modern version of nihilism in fact finds refuge in a formal rationality which ignores or destroys meaning while erecting ever more complex systems. Multileveled formal systems of increasing complexity are elaborated which remain the same whatever the subject matter. A formal system as such is indifferent to the material content or subject matter, which may be of the utmost triviality or of outstanding importance, meaningful or meaningless. The social counterpart to a nihilistic indifference to any meaning or intelligibility other than that of formal systems is a dictatorship of bureaucrats, who run society as a system without reference to substantive values or ends. Their rule is accepted passively by many, because the only alternative would seem to be the imposition of a self-styled unchanging set of beliefs and values by some external authority, and ancestral memories of the suppression of freedom make people prefer, though without enthusiasm, the rule of technocrats and bureaucrats. That preference, however, may prove catastrophically disastrous when the formal system is that of war games, now played with nuclear weapons.

Symbolism and figurative speech, it seems to me, may occupy the middle ground between metaphysics and nihilism. Symbols are meaningful. They do have a reference. They embody not simply the subjective side of human experience but the intentionality of that experience in its movement towards and insight into objective reality. At the same time, symbols do not leave the subject in a stance of theoretical contemplation of reality but engage the subject in a practical involvement with it. The subjectivism for which symbolism is often blamed is at least in part a practical relationship of the subject with reality in the concrete, rather than with the contemplation of its abstract form or essence. However, while symbols do have objective referents, their mode of reference is flexible. They are polysemous, carrying a plurality of meanings, not merely successively but simultaneously. They are not imperialistic, and the use of one particular symbol or set of symbols does not exclude the existence of equivalent symbols, serving more or less the same function. It is a question of overlapping rather than of identical meaning, but symbol sets may exist in a complementary relationship, without one set trying to exclude the others by making exclusive claims as carriers of meaning.

Now it is my contention that a recognition that symbolism is the appropriate mode of knowledge and expression for substantive questions of meaning and value in relation to human existence can preserve society from a destructive swing between metaphysics and nihilism, between oppression and empty freedom, and allow the development of a pluralistic world order with the convergence and complementarity of diverse cultures. Pluralism is not the same as relativism. Relativism is the trivialization of content that accompanies the dominance of formal rationality and the attempt to compress all human meaning in the straitjacket of formal systems. Pluralism is the response of finite intelligence to a reality so rich that it constantly escapes its categories and calls for the convergence and complementarity of various cultures and modes of expression.

That does not mean that anything goes, that any old symbol or figure will do at all times and in all places. Symbols lose their validity, because they no longer relate the subject truly and effectively to the real situation. They become cognitively false as provoking false judgments and practically harmful. The imagination has the constant task of constructing, deconstructing, and reconstructing the language of symbols, so that these may mediate our changing experience. To examine the working of the imagination in relation to the Christian religion, so as to open the way to the new developments the present situation demands, is my purpose here.

CHAPTER 1

The Structure of the Religious Imagination

If religion is taken in its external reality in society and history, it may be defined as "a set of symbolic forms and acts that relate man to the ultimate conditions of his existence."[6] What I want to do is to examine the structure and working of the Christian religion as a symbol system. However, it would be a mistake to begin with the presupposition that the Christian religion is a single symbol system. Both the history of the Christian religion and the study of its manifestations in any given period uncover the variety of symbol systems the Christian religion has always included. No doubt every form of the Christian religion draws upon the common stock of Christian symbols, handed down in the Christian tradition. But the individual symbols—like words, their chief vehicle—derive their meaning in any actual instance from the relationships they bear to one another when organized into a complex whole, just as words derive their actual meaning from their place in a sentence and a sentence from its place in a composition or work. If, then, we ask, What is the Christian religion? we shall receive several different answers according to how the religious data are construed and organized into one or other complex, meaningful whole.

The task of moulding the manifold of religious phenomena—signs, words, institutions, actions—into a symbol system under some governing idea or shaping principle may be assigned to the religious imagination. Religion in the concrete as a set of symbols meaningfully organized is a product of the imagination, the name usually given to the function and activity of consciousness by which we work up the buzzing, confused manifold of experience into ordered unities and sets. The task of the imagination in selecting items as data and organizing unified wholes from the ceaseless stream of experience is prior to logical analysis and rational explanation, inasmuch as it constructs the objects on which those functions are exercised.

A question arises here concerning the objectivity of our knowledge. It is being raised today in relation to language particularly and the use of signs generally. Is language (and other sign processes) the conferring of meaning upon otherwise meaningless experiential material, or is it the discovery or at any rate the actualization of prior meaning or potential meaning? Are all cultural products and systems the imposition of fictive meaning upon what is meaningless in itself? Is all meaning a fiction, arbitrary at its basis? To put it in another way: Do linguistic utterances or written statements or other sign products refer to any reality outside of themselves, to some nonlinguistic order of things? Some, like Jacques Derrida, deny that they do. The meaning of signs they contend, is constituted not by a reference to an objective, unmediated real world but by their relation to other signs within the same sign system. There is an endless play of significations but no final meaning, because there is no order of reality outside the language or sign system which can limit the free play of linguistic or sign meanings.

How far then does the imagination create the meanings it organizes into a symbolic system? The question is a misleading one. After all, the whole knowing process is creative insofar as all knowledge is the product of human intelligence and reflects the reality of the knowing subject, not just the reality of the object known. Knowledge is not the passive imprinting of an external reality upon the mind but the active struggle of the mind to assimilate and transform that reality into a cognitive content of percepts, images, ideas, concepts, propositions, related to other items in a body of knowledge. We grasp in a new knowing what we can somehow relate to our previous knowledge. Knowledge is always shaped by the knowing subject; it is never the unmodified imprint of a preexisting object. The question, therefore, should be not, How far does the mind or imagination create its meanings? but, How far can the meanings it creates be verified in reality? There is no simple answer, because meanings are of different kinds. Some, like those of the natural sciences, are the product of the mind's attempt to master reality as independent of it; others, like those embodied in legal and political institutions, such as a law court or parliament, are the result of an attempt to create and give permanence to a human world of society and culture, a world having no reality independently of the human creation of meaning.

There is not an exact correspondence between the order of words and the order of things, between the order of thought and the order of reality. The precise relationship between the two has to be determined in any particular instance by a critical judgment, grounded reflectively upon the data. There is in any event a subjective, creative, constructive element in all our knowledge, which is why we speak of the imagination, the scientific imagination as well as the religious imagination. Further, our knowing is always qualified by the language or sign system within which it occurs. Language is a medium in and through which we know reality and create our world, the world in which we live. We cannot separate our knowledge and our world from their linguistic expression and live in a relationship with reality unmediated by language. To ask for a direct access to a nonlinguistic reality is like asking for a nature unmodified by human action. Nature and the results of human activity are inextricably interwoven, and in our approach to nature we act upon it. Likewise language and our experience and knowledge of reality are inseparable, and insofar as we reach a nonlinguistic reality, we do so through language. Nevertheless the recognition of the function of the shaping spirit or imagination and of the complex interpenetration of thought and language does not, it seems to me, justify us in enclosing the human mind within a labyrinth of language with no exit, so that meanings endlessly wind back upon themselves and lead nowhere. The denial that language or sign systems have any reference to reality is a form of nihilism, which opts for ultimate meaninglessness, declaring that all our meanings are in the last analysis arbitrary, like the linguistic signs themselves.

The question, however, of the referential function of language is peculiarly complicated in the case of religious language.[7]

In the first place, religious language is evocative language. As Ian Ramsey has argued,[8] the function of religious language is to provoke the occurrence of a disclosure. I myself would explain the matter in this way. Faith is an intentional experience, in the Husserlian sense of intentionality, which Husserl himself borrowed from Brentano, who derived it from the Scholastic tradition. That means that faith is an experience of some reality; it intends a reality; it puts us into contact with what reveals itself in the experience as its term. Faith is not a merely subjective experience in the sense that the subject is enclosed within his or her own states without reaching any reality beyond them. Just as all consciousness as intentional is consciousness *of* something, so also faith as intentional is the experience *of* the reality felt in the darkness that surrounds human existence. But that formulation already points to the peculiarity of faith. The reality experienced in faith does not manifest itself as an object. It reveals itself as the term of a feeling response but remains hidden from us or unknown inasmuch as it does not appear to consciousness as an apprehensible object. I have elsewhere[9] in some detail expounded the nature of feeling as distinguished both from intellectual apprehension and from emotion. Briefly, feelings rest upon a oneness between the subject and what is felt. Unlike intellectual activity and emotional reaction, each in its own way a partial, restricted response, feeling is a total response, that is, a response of our total being, intelligent and bodily, spiritual and material. Feelings are responses springing from what we are. They are responses of our being to reality as we meet it. Our feeling-responses depend upon what we have become as beings, what we are as persons. Feelings are the resonance of reality upon human subjects, the arousal of our personal being through union with a reality present to us. In the case of religious feeling, the response of our spiritual affectivity to transcendent reality precedes knowledge and continues without any direct knowledge of a kind that would make the term of that response a known object. The reality that draws us where our own being falls off into nothingness, the reality that gives a sense of basic fulfilment at the center of our emptiness, remains outside our intellectual grasp. Where we are dealing with known objects, the language we use conveys information about them to one another, and this information can be registered by the mind without any arousal of our personal being or engagement of our spiritual affectivity. The language of faith concerning transcendent reality has no such information to convey. Therefore, if the language does not evoke a personal response of faith, it remains language without any apparent reference, expressing merely a subjective state. Or, to adopt another approach, its referent may with Feuerbach and Durkheim be taken as human reality or society, though cloaked by religious images. Hence, if the language of faith is to communicate its true content, it must provoke a disclosure through the arousal of faith.

In the second place, the language of faith is always symbolic. Besides evoking the experience of faith, religious language also serves to articulate that experience. Now any intentional experience is specified by its object. In other words, we define a state of consciousness by determining what it is a consciousness of. With faith, however, the term of the experience, that of which faith is a consciousness, remains unknown. The experience of faith cannot therefore be directly specified or described. Consequently the language of faith is always metaphoric in that wider sense in which metaphor is speaking of one thing in terms of another[10] and is tied to symbols, namely to expressive elements (images, concepts, words, stories) with a double intentionality, referring directly to one thing and through it, indirectly, analogically, to another.

Let me elaborate that. All religious images, concepts, words, statements, stories, I say, have a double intentionality, namely, a double level of sense and reference. As used religiously they express and refer to transcendent reality or mystery. But because there is no direct apprehension of the term of faith, which remains unknown or hidden as mystery, their immediate level of meaning and reference, that which provides all their imaginative and ideational content, is within the world of finite objects, the world of our everyday experience. Language used religiously is always taken from some area of our ordinary, nonreligious experience. Its usage becomes religious when its immediate, secular sense and reference is rendered inoperative by some device or other. Its direct interpretation is made implausible or inconsequential, so that the language must either be dismissed as meaningless and empty of reference or interpreted as having a deeper meaning and pointing towards mystery. The immediate sense and reference are not entirely removed; they remain as functioning symbolically, as providing the content for an indirect or symbolic expression of the directly inexpressible mystery. Various procedures or devices are used to shift language from its immediate functioning to a symbolic function. I may mention Ricoeur's treatment of extravagance and intensification in parables and proverbs[11] and Ian Ramsey's examination of qualifiers.[12] Something in the language or context prevents one from taking what is said in its ordinary meaning and leads one to a symbolic interpretation. For example, the language of ancient kingship is used in the Bible of God. All the imaginative and ideational content comes from what was said about kings in those days but now used in such an absolute and unlimited fashion as to be inapplicable to any earthly king. The hyperbole for once is to be taken seriously.

In the third place, religious language is not exclusively concerned with the transcendent term of the movement of faith. The experience of transcendent reality reaches out over the whole of human experience and pervades the interpretation of finite things. There thus arises a religious interpretation of humanity, of human action, of society and culture, of history, of nature, of the material universe. That religious interpretation is set forth in sets of religious beliefs. Such beliefs are propositions expressing judgments of fact and judgments of value, made under the influence of the experience of faith. While these propositional beliefs belong to the symbolic context of faith and to the language of faith and depend upon that context for their full intelligibility and grounding, some of them—not all—are straightforward literal factual assertions or moral precepts. Because of the integration of religious experience into a cultural matrix, religious language is thus wider than the language of faith in the strict sense.

But, in the fourth place, we should not overstress the part of factual beliefs in religion. Religious language is to a great extent an example of poetic language, insofar as its reference is not to the factual reality of the existing world but to possible worlds envisioned by the poetic imagination. Religious language is not primarily a description of reality to be formulated in factual beliefs but a redescription of reality under the movement of desire, opening us out to new worlds of possible experience. In that sense there is in religious language a suspension of reference to present reality.

Fifthly, and last in this analysis of the referential function of religious language, I come to the complete symbol systems, constructed by the religious imagination. These weld together all the elements already mentioned and present an entire attitude towards God, humanity, and the universe. Needless to say, such a symbol system is not a simple transcription of the order of reality, any more than a scientific theory is a simple transcription of physical data. A symbol system, like a scientific theory, is a construct of the human mind, not indeed an arbitrary invention, but dependent all the same upon the selection, not necessarily deliberately thought out, of one from several possible paradigms.

As I have already remarked, in the Christian tradition there has been and still is a variety of symbol systems. These represent different answers to the question, What is the Christian religion? At the origin of each is the choice of a different governing idea or shaping principle for the organization of the Christian symbolic material. The comparative merit of each symbol system as an interpretative model for the Christian religion demands discussion. The criteria for assessing the relative validity of a Christian symbol system will be, on the first level, its fidelity and comprehensiveness in relation to the data of the Christian tradition, and, on the second level, its adequacy as a religious paradigm to human experience. All the same, these symbol systems need not be taken as mutually exclusive. Each may be seen as preserving insights neglected or at least not fully developed in the others. The dominance of one model at a particular time may lead to a onesidedness that is corrected by a shift to another, which in its turn leads to a onesidedness calling for correction in a different direction. Several reasons make it unlikely that a single symbol system will ever satisfy all needs. The reasons I have in mind are the contradictory features of human experience, such as unmerited suffering on the one hand and the joyful goodness of life on the other; the variety and at least partial equivalence of available religious symbols; the comprehensive sweep demanded of a religious tradition as concerning the ultimate conditions of human existence. All that points to what we actually find in Christian history, namely, the coexistence and successive dominance of different symbol systems, partly complementary, partly in conflict.

The hypothesis I am now going to develop is that there are four major forms of the Christian religion, four symbol systems or interpretative models under which the Christian symbolic material has been organized by the religious imagination.

CHAPTER 2

Four Generative Ideas and Four Master Tropes

Four different ideas may be used as shaping principles to organize the Christian material into a symbol system. Each idea may be seen as generating a particular form of the Christian religion. The first idea is that of the Whole, that is, the idea of a total order as normative. This generates the type of Christianity I shall call mythical. The second idea is that of praxis; in other words, the Christian religion is conceived as a practical way of life. This generates the pragmatic form of the Christian religion. The third idea is the distinction between two worlds, the present world of sin and corruption and the future world, hidden at present and still to be made manifest, but here already now in the elect or chosen few. This generates what may be called the visionary type of Christianity. The fourth idea is that of an unmediated experience of the Godhead. It gives rise to the mystical form of the Christian religion. Thus:

Idea	Total order as normative	Practical way of life	Two worlds	Unmediated experience of Godhead
Type of Christian religion	Mythical	Pragmatic	Visionary	Mystical

What I am doing is constructing four ideal types of the Christian religion. The word "ideal" has not, as those familiar with Max Weber's usage will know, any normative implication. Ideal types are hypothetical constructions, which are composed from the empirical and historical data to serve as heuristic devices in making comparisons and reaching explanations of the material under investigation.

Another way of designating the four versions of the Christian religion would be to speak of four traditions of discourse. The word "discourse" here means the manner in which the material of sign processes is handled and organized. To speak of a "tradition" of discourse is to indicate the historical dimension, according to which one or other kind of discourse becomes dominant in a particular period. Most suggestive here is Timothy Reiss's account[13] of the shift in the seventeenth century from a discourse of patterning, roughly corresponding to my mythical type of the Christian religion, to an analytico-referential tradition of discourse, which, as I shall argue, relates to my pragmatic and mystical types. We may also think here of Foucault's notion of "episteme", namely, of a basic structure of all knowledge in a given period[14] though I should want to interpret this less rigidly as indicating the dominance of a particular episteme, without affirming, as Foucault does, the impossibility of thinking outside the episteme of one's period.

My four ideal types thus do have an historical dimension. Since they are constructed from the historical data, they are helpful in understanding the shifts that have occurred in Christian history. Moreover, the four types do stand in a sequential relationship to one another, so that they suggest a basic cycle through which religious consciousness passes in its effort to organize the religious data. Nevertheless, though the four types may be seen as articulating the basic rhythm of consciousness underlying historical development, it would be a great oversimplification of the complexities of history to interpret them as stages of Christian history. Though one or other of them may be dominant in a given period, they are permanent forms which the Christian religion may take at any time, and several are always found existing simultaneously. In short, to use current jargon, my approach is primarily synchronic, not diachronic. I am concerned with the different possibilities available to the religious imagination as it works the religious data into an overall symbol system.

My reflection has been greatly stimulated at this point by Hayden White's analysis of the deep structure of the historical imagination,[15] and, since his analysis uncovers the modes of human consciousness, it can, it seems to me, be fruitfully applied to the religious imagination. However, let me say at the outset that my concern here is not with a faithful exposition of Hayden White's view but with using the insights I have culled from him for my own analysis of the forms of the Christian religion. While I am not conscious of having distorted his views in any major respect, the transfer I am making clearly involves judgments that might not be acceptable to Hayden White.

White distinguishes four principal modes of historical consciousness. Each of these proceeds by exploiting one of four kinds of figuration. The four basic kinds of figuration or, in Kenneth Burke's phrase, "master tropes,"[16] were identified in post-Renaissance theory of rhetoric as metaphor, metonymy, synecdoche, and irony. Vico, in particular, argued that those were the four principal tropes from which all figures of speech are derived. He saw them as the basis for understanding the cycles through which consciousness passes in trying to understand a world that lies beyond our capacity to know it fully; and he also used the four tropes in developing his theory of the cycle of four stages through which all civilizations pass.[17]

For Hayden White the four terms, metaphor, metonymy, synecdoche and irony, which in their proper sense refer to particular figures of speech, stand in a transferred sense for four basic tropological strategies, which determine the mode of figuration underlying and informing an historical work. There are, in other words, four basic modes of prefiguration, understanding prefiguration to mean the prior selection of a figural mode to be used in construing the relevant field of phenomena and working up the data into objects for representation, analysis, and explanation. What Hayden White postulates is a deep, precritical level of consciousness on which the historian performs an essentially poetic act. That act is the selection of a basic mode of figuration or tropological strategy by which he prefigures the historical field and constitutes as an object domain on which he can then exercise the manifest functions of the historian.

My hypothesis is that the religious imagination has a similar structure. There is a deep, precritical level on which in an essentially poetic act a basic mode of figuration is selected, and this determines the manner in which the religious sign material is organized into a symbolic system. But before examining their application to the religious imagination, we must look more closely at the four master tropes.

Metaphor is the original way a domain of experience is encoded. Phenomena are characterized in terms of similarity or difference and thus united to one another in a pattern or whole. In relation to the underlying, literal level of meaning, which the figurative language is endeavouring to grasp, metaphor is essentially representational. In other words, where the contents of experience resist direct expression, they are figuratively encoded through analogy, which means by identification with what on account of some similarity or resemblance represents them.

However, the metaphorical encoding of experience through similarity and difference sets up a tension between language and reality, which leads to a movement of decoding or deconstruction in a struggle for further refinements of language. The first move in that direction is the dissolution of the metaphoric pattern or totality into its elements and their characterization simply in terms of their contiguity or juxtaposition in space and time. Here we meet the basic trope of metonymy. As a figure of speech, metonymy is the transference of a name from one feature to another simply because they are contiguously associated. Contiguity here means the relation items have to one another in the same context. In metonymy the name of one item is used to stand for another item in that context or for the whole contexture or combination of items. Thus: "Downing St.," the name of the official residence, is made to stand for the British Prime Minister and her functions, "cup" and "dish" for their contents, "sail" for the whole ship, "the turf" for horse racing, and so on. If we now consider metonymy not as a mere figure of speech but as a tropological strategy or figural mode, it is the construal of a domain of experience in a set of part-part relationships, where the whole is reduced to its parts or elements. Hence in its relation to the underlying, literal level of meaning, metonymy uses figurative language in a reductionist fashion, insofar as it breaks up the metaphorical whole into an analytical description of its elements according to their relationships of merely spatial and temporal contiguity.

That analysis of the original metaphoric pattern into its elements, however, uncovers more than simple part-part relationships. There emerges the relationship where the part is an attribute or quality that can characterize the whole, that symbolizes, as it were, the essence of the whole. Where a part thus symbolizes the whole we have the third trope, synecdoche. Synecdoche is usually taken as a form of metonymy, but there is a difference. Metonymy reduces the whole to its parts: synecdoche finds the quality or essence of the whole in the parts. "Fifty sail" for "fifty ships"—a metonymy—reduces a whole to its part; "He is all heart"—a synecdoche—takes the quality of the part as constituting the essential nature of the whole. Likewise, the use of "capital" to designate those who own and control the means of production takes the part of our economic system that determines and hence symbolizes its essential structure and thus is a synecdoche rather than a metonymy. Thus, in relation to the underlying, literal meaning, which the figurative language is trying to grasp, synecdoche as a basic figural mode is integrative, in the sense of intrinsically relating the parts within a whole. It is a partial return to the metaphoric totality, but where that totality does not come first, where, instead, the movement is from the particular or part to the universal or whole.

Finally comes irony, which as a tropological strategy sees the contrast and opposition hidden within every apparent resemblance or unity. It focuses upon the inadequacy of all language and is the capacity to say one thing and mean another, to mean one thing and say it in a number of alternative, mutually exclusive, and illogical ways. Irony gives rise to a number of particular figures of speech, such as catachresis (a manifestly absurd expression), for example, "blind mouths," and oxymoron (the conjunction of contradictory elements), as in "cold passion". The relation of irony to the underlying, literal level of meaning is negational, because it denies on the figurative level what is affirmed on the literal level. With it the deconstruction of the original metaphoric whole into its elements has come to an end in ironic reflection upon the inadequacy of all encoding. But deconstruction thus negates itself and leads to a turning back to metaphoric patterning as a way out of the impasse, but now with recognition of the constructive element in all expression.

To recapitulate, then: Underlying as a deep structure any symbol system is a figural mode. There are four figural modes. The original encoding of experience is metaphorical. This gives rise to analysis into elements, which at first is reductionist, resulting in a metonymic interpretation of parts in terms of mere contiguity. Out of that comes the recognition of parts as symbolizing the essence of the totality, a strategy we call synecdoche. However, the reductionist trend pushes through the integration achieved by synecdoche into an ironic acknowledgment of the limitations and contradictions present in all modes of encoding experience.

The sequential order in which these basic tropes are arranged corresponds to the vector of tension that relates them to one another. It is not to be supposed that either individual or communal consciousness always passes through them all in a process of development. Nor should they without much further elaboration be taken as historical stages. In their essential meaning they are four basic modes of human consciousness, precritical and metalogical, four ways of articulating a basic structure in relation to which experience can be constituted as an ordered domain, capable of being handled by specific procedures of objective knowledge.

In adopting through the mediation of Hayden White the traditional fourfold classification of master tropes, I have left aside the more recent but very influential bipolar analysis of language put forward by Roman Jakobson.[18] According to Jakobson, all linguistic signs are formed by a twofold process: the *selection* of parts from the available inventory or storehouse of the language and the *combination* of these parts into a sequence. The selective process operates by similarity, the combinative process by contiguity, so that the two processes correspond to metaphor and metonymy. Hence those two basic rhetorical figures, metaphor and metonymy, represent the fundamental bipolarity or cardinal dichotomy in language between its vertical, associative, synchronic relations and its horizontal, combinative or syntagmatic, diachronic relations. Jakobson's analysis is supported by his studies of aphasia, which led him to distinguish two types of speech disturbance, namely, similarity disorder and contiguity disorder. In similarity disorder only the combinative side of language was preserved, whereas in contiguity disorder there was an inability to handle syntactic rules, so that speech was limited to substituting words by similarities.

I have no wish to contest the validity of Jakobson's bipolar analysis. It is simply less useful to my present purpose than the traditional fourfold classification. The two analyses need not however be opposed. The four master tropes may be brought under the two processes by putting synecdoche under metaphor and irony under metonymy. Admittedly Jakobson himself sees synecdoche as an instance of metonymy, and the term is often applied in a manner that supports that identification. But I have restricted synecdoche to instances where the part stands for the whole not because of contiguity alone but because of some quality that in some fashion represents or symbolizes the whole and that brings it under the metaphoric process of substitution. As for irony, it may well be seen as the dominance to the extreme of dissonance or absurdity of the combinatory process of metonymy over the similarity process of metaphor.

To return, then to the fourfold classification of figural modes. There is a correspondence between the four forms or ideal types of the Christian religion I have listed above and the four master tropes. The mythical type of Christian religion, generated by the idea of a total order as normative, corresponds to the trope of metaphor. Myth creates a totality or whole by patterning experience through relations of similarity or difference. The second, pragmatic type of Christian religion arises when the tropological strategy of metonymy has reduced the metaphoric whole into its elements. Since these elements—symbolic, doctrinal, institutional, ritual—are related to one another simply in part-part relationships and in terms of historical or spatial (geographical) contiguity, they are unable to define the Christian religion. The defining characteristic becomes the pragmatic one of Christianity as a moral way of life. Religion is reduced to ethics, and the symbolic elements are seen as subserving moral practice. That reduction, however, uncovers the truth that Christian practice does not find its meaning in the context of this world. Christian life is a life lived under the vision of a world to come. The symbolic elements are now interpreted as allegories of the world lying hidden behind the world of appearances. Thus there arises the visionary type of Christian religion, corresponding to the figural mode of synecdoche. But the thrust towards deconstruction continues and uncovers the limits and inadequacy of all language and expression. Insofar as religious faith survives the critique of the ironic mode, it does so in the form of mystical experience that negates the finite meaning of every expression it itself uses.

We may therefore expand the previous table:

Type of Christian religion	Mythical	Pragmatic	Visionary	Mystical
Basic tropes	Metaphor	Metonymy	Synecdoche	Irony
Relation to underlying literal meaning	Representational	Reductionist	Integrative	Negational

The four forms of the Christian religion I have distinguished correspond to the four senses of Scripture in the medieval tradition. This brings the four senses of Scripture into a parallelism with the four basic tropes, and confirms that with those tropes we are dealing with fundamental modes of the constructive imagination.

Medieval writers distinguished these four senses: the literal or historical, the tropological or moral, the allegorical, and the anagogical or mystical.

For the medievals, the literal sense was the primary meaning as expressed by the words of the text; it therefore corresponds to the fundamental encoding of Christian experience as myth—historical myth. It might seem strange to align the literal or historical sense with metaphor and the mythical form of Christianity, but closer consideration removes the paradox. First, the medievals themselves acknowledged that the primary or literal sense of the text was sometimes metaphorical. Second, it is Hayden White's hypothesis, which I am putting to use here, that underlying all historical narrative is a prefigurative act or tropological strategy, so that all history at the deep level is metaphorical, inasmuch as all the basic tropes are forms of metaphor. Third, the realistic narratives of the Bible are historylike, rather than historical in the modern sense, so that they constitute an elaboration and patterning of the events narrated into a metaphoric representation of the religious experience of the People of God. For those three reasons, it is not contradictory to regard the literal or historical sense of the medieval classification as corresponding to the fundamental encoding of religious experience according to the figural mode of metaphor and thus corresponding to the mythical type of the Christian religion.

The other three senses, called spiritual senses by the medievals, correspond clearly enough to the other three types of Christian religion: the tropological or moral to the pragmatic type, the allegorical to the visionary type, and the anagogical to the mystical type. Hence they parallel the three basic tropes of metonymy, synecdoche, and irony.

Besides identifying the deep structure of the historical imagination by distinguishing its four principal modes according to the four basic kinds of figuration or master tropes, Hayden White analyzes the manifest dimensions of an historical work. He gives these as aesthetic, epistemological, and moral. The aesthetic dimension is constituted by emplotment, which shapes the historical narrative and gives it meaning by plotting it as a particular kind of story. Epistemologically an historical work uses different kinds of formal argument; and its moral dimension is its reflection of the ideological stance of the historian, that is, his or her prescriptive assumptions concerning present social reality and practice. Thus there are three constituents of historical style on the manifest level, namely, emplotment, formal argument, and ideological implication.

Each of these is then given a fourfold articulation. Following Northrop Frye,[19] Hayden White distinguishes four possible modes of emplotment: comedy, tragedy, romance, and satire. He takes over from Stephen Pepper[20] a distinction of four basic forms of philosophical argument: organicist, mechanistic, formist, and contextualist. Modifying Karl Mannheim's analysis,[21] he lists four possible modes of ideological implication: conservative, liberal, radical, and anarchist.

Hayden White then arranges those three sets of four into parallel columns and sees, not a necessary combination, but an elective affinity between the items that fall horizontally together on each line of the columns. Thus, although other combinations are possible, there is, for example, an elective affinity relating a comic emplotment, an organicist mode of argument and a conservative ideology. White's account of these affinities and his application of the analysis to the historiography and philosophy of history of the nineteenth century is subtle and detailed. For him the effort to combine a mode of emplotment with a form of argument or an ideological implication inconsonant with it sets up a dialectical tension, such as characterizes the work of every great historian.

My own application of these sets of distinctions is going to be much simpler. Although I know this may seem crude in relation to White's subtlety, I want to relate each form of the Christian religion I have distinguished to a particular mode of emplotment, a particular form of argument, and a particular ideological implication. In doing so, I recognize that the combinations are not necessary but express only an affinity. Historically we shall find hybrid types. I am also aware that, unlike Hayden White, I am relating the deep and the manifest structures of consciousness in a direct fashion and thereby running the risk of creating a rigid formalism. Nevertheless, although the combinations I shall put forward are neither logically nor psychologically necessary, they reflect sufficiently strong affinities to allow us to fill out the four ideal types of Christian religion with which we began this analysis. Those four ideal types, thus expanded, will, I suggest, prove useful heuristic tools in investigating the past history and possible future transformations of the Christian religion.

So the first version of Christian religion, the mythical, which encodes experience by constructing a representational totality or normative order, usually plots the Christian story as a comedy. In a comedy the story heads towards reconciliation and ends happily with the harmony of all with all. When the Christian story is emplotted as a comedy, the drama of the fall and redemption and of the crucifixion and resurrection are inserted into the wider theme of creation and restoration, which softens the dualistic and tragic elements.

In the second version of Christian religion, the pragmatic, when the

Christian myth has been broken up into its elements, the Christian story is predominantly read as a tragedy. If comedy is a presentation of things as they should be and thus of ultimate harmony, tragedy is the disclosure of things as they actually are and of the impossibility of resolving all oppositions. Tragedy tells a story of the conflict between good and good, rather than between good and evil. When the Christian religion is reduced to moral practice, it loses its festive tone and takes on a note of resignation as humankind bends before the unalterably opposed elements affecting its existence. The Christian religion becomes faithful service in imitation of Christ and in obedience to his teaching and perseverance in a situation of unresolved conflict, following the example of the crucified Jesus.

The plot structure of the third version of Christian religion, the visionary, is that of romance. Romance is the story of the successful quest, with a crucial conflict between the hero and an enemy, with a vision of final victory. As Hayden White puts it, romance is "a drama of the triumph of good over evil, of virtue over vice, of light over darkness, and of the ultimate transcendence of man over the world in which he was imprisoned by the Fall."[22]

It may seem somewhat farfetched to link the fourth version of Christian religion, the mystical, to satire, which is the plot structure corresponding to the figural mode of irony. I admit there is a measure of artificiality, as there is bound to be with any formal analysis. Nevertheless, a unity of presupposition binds mysticism to satire and makes the parallelism meaningful. Satire expresses the ultimate inadequacy of any human response to the chaos and confusion of life in this world. It frustrates the resolution offered by the other three kinds of plot. This relates it closest to tragedy. But it refuses even the resolution through moral action, sought by the pragmatic version of Christian religion. The insights of satire and the knowledge of mysticism stand apart from any relevance to social and cultural problems. For satire as for mysticism, the world has grown old, and the awareness found in each version of the inadequacy of its own image of reality leads to a turning back to myth and the metaphoric mode. The affinity between satire and mysticism is exemplified in T.S. Eliot's transition from *The Waste Land* to *The Four Quartets.*

I turn now to the modes of formal argument, where I draw directly upon Stephen Pepper's *World Hypotheses,* though adapting his account to suit my own purpose. He distinguishes four modes: organicist, mechanistic, formist, and contextualist. In the way they handle the data, the first two are integrative or synthetic and the second two dispersive or analytic.

The organicist mode of discourse or form of philosophical reflection tends to consolidate particulars into wholes greater than the sum of the individual parts. The root metaphor underlying the argumentation is the depiction of reality as organic process. Hence in seeking causes, stress falls upon finality as operative throughout the universe. There is a clear affinity between this mode of discourse and the mythical elaboration of the Christian religion with its comic plot.

Mechanistic discourse, though integrative in binding particulars together, is reductionistic. Its concern is with laws and functions, not with wholes. Underneath the argumentation lies the root metaphor of the machine or set of merely functionally related parts. It seeks to determine cause-effect relationships, that is, efficient causes. An affinity links mechanistic discourse with the metonymic construal of experience as a set of part-part relationships and with the pragmatic or, in other words, functional interpretation of Christian religion. Mechanicism shares with the tragic emplotment the sense of disclosing reality as it actually is without cloaking it in an overall finality or comic resolution.

The formist mode of argument does not place particulars in a network of laws, but considers them in their particularity. In that sense it is dispersive. But because it proceeds by analyzing the intrinsic qualities of those particulars, it uncovers the similarities and differences that relate them to one another. It therefore moves towards integration. The underlying root metaphor is that of a work of art. The autonomy of a work of art corresponds to the dispersive character of formism; the relation that binds works of art together in a tradition or school parallels formism's movement towards integration. As the name indicates, formism investigates formal causes. There is an affinity with the visionary version of the Christian religion, with its distinction between the world of appearances and the real world to come. Particular elements of this world are revealed in their intrinsic meaning when they are interpreted as so many manifestations of the ideal forms of the new world beneath the veil. The focus of the formist mode is on the individual symbols, in contrast to the mythical interpretation, which emphasizes the whole.

The contextualist mode of discourse has as its root metaphor the event. Something happened, and the argument proceeds by tracing back the threads that link the event in various directions to the context until those threads disperse ever more widely and disappear into what for human apprehension is a limitless background. No cause is sought other than the material cause of insertion into a context. The mode of argumentation suits irony and satire as the refusal of any resolution of conflict or any achievement of reconciliation; and it also harmonizes with the mystical pursuit of every line of thought into an inapprehensible abyss or absence of human meaning.

The third and last dimension of the work of the constructive imagination on the manifest level is the moral, which may be identified with the ideological implication of the completed symbol system. As I have already noted, Hayden White distinguishes four possible modes of ideological implication: conservative, liberal, radical and anarchist. (Here I differ from him in my account of these modes and in discerning the affinities between them and the other elements already discussed.)

Ideology—to recall my previous definition—is the set of prescriptive assumptions concerning social reality and practice; in other words, it is the metapolitical stance that governs concrete political judgements and action. The fundamental principle of conservative ideology is that there is a prior normative order. There are undoubtedly various kinds of conservatisms, distinguished, for example, according to whether the prior order is interpreted as a static system or as a dynamic, developing process. Nevertheless, all conservatives look to some prior order as norm. The mythical form of Christian religion, with its comic emplotment and its organicist argumentation, favors a conservative ideology. Liberalism as an ideology assumes a plurality of orders, existing in mutual toleration because grounded practically not theoretically. It corresponds to the moral or pragmatic version of the Christian religion, and has an affinity with the latter's tragic plot, which sees conflict as between good and good, and with mechanistic argumentation, which looks for functional relationships. Radicalism's fundamental principle is that there is a new order to be created out of the destruction of the old. It is the ideology of visionary Christianity, with its dualism of old and new worlds, the formist argumentation which that occasions, and the emplotment of the Christian story as romance, namely as a transcendent conflict, leading to the triumph of good over evil. Finally, for anarchism there is no order outside the individual, and this echoes the individualism and contextualism of the mystical version of the Christian religion, with its ironical rejection of all attempts to discern an order in the confusion of the finite world.

It will now, I think, be helpful to present the foregoing analysis with its correspondences in a table:

Type of Christian religion	Mythical: total order as normative	Pragmatic: practical way of life	Visionary: new world in contrast to the old	Mystical: unmediated experience of the Absolute
Basic trope	Metaphor: representational	Metonymy: reductionist	Synecdoche: integrative	Irony: negational
Senses of Scripture	literal or historical	tropological or moral	allegorical	anagogical or mystical
Emplotment	Comic: ultimate harmony of all with all	Tragic: ultimate disclosure of things as they are; conflict of good with good	Romance: vision of ultimate victory of good over evil	Satire: ultimate inadequacy of human response to life in this chaotic world

Argumentation	Organicist: integrative discourse based on root metaphor of organic process. Stresses finality	Mechanistic: integrative but reductionistic discourse, searching for laws and functions. Root-metaphor: machine	Formism: dispersive discourse but relating particulars to one another. Root metaphor: work of art	Contextualism: dispersive discourse based on root metaphor of event and tracing its antecedents back into limitless context
Ideological implication	Conservatism: prior order as normative	Liberalism: a plurality of pragmatic orders	Radicalism: new order to be created	Anarchism: no order outside the individual

What I now wish to do is, in four successive sections, to give a positive exposition of each version of the Christian religion, a more concrete presentation than the abstract outlines I have so far sketched. Then in a further four sections I will proceed to a critique of each version, pointing out its limitations, its possible distortions of Christian truth and value, and its potential for further development in the future.

CHAPTER 3

First Model: Mythical Christianity

The first model or ideal type of Christian religion I am calling mythical. By myth here I mean a comprehensive account of the order of the world, of society and of the nature and destiny of the individual. A myth is in the first place a cosmology. It turns the chaos and buzzing confusion of reality as we experience it into a cosmos or ordered whole. It may or may not include a cosmogony or an account of how the cosmos came to be, but it must at least establish reality as a cosmos or ordered world. In a myth society is presented as part of the cosmic order. Myth, therefore, serves as a social charter. The institutions, laws, and customs of society are legitimized by referring them to the myth. Not every element need be regarded as having equal value, and for some functions there is the possibility of alternatives. But taken as a whole the social order reflects the cosmic order, is a part of it, and consequently is not open to fundamental change. The nature of the individual reflects the cosmic order; the human being is a microcosm within the macrocosm. The destiny of the individual has to be worked out under the conditions and norms of the total order.

The myth is seen as presenting reality as it actually is. *This,* it is taken for granted, is the true account of the world and humanity as they are; alternative accounts are false or at the most only partially true. The myth is thus interpreted as a realistic account. One could say that the myth is taken literally, meaning that it is taken as the inherently appropriate, the proper, expression of the objective order of reality. But that meaning of the literal does not exclude the metaphorical use of language. The one order includes languages as well as things. Things and words are brought together under one overarching totality. Words have an essential and inherent relationship with things. They are not arbitrary signs. Knowledge and discourse are not conceived as the mastery and manipulation of objects over against the subject but as the uncovering and articulation of a pattern of relationships within a totality to which subjects, objects, things, and words all equally belong. Hence, since the total pattern is one of resemblances and correspondences, of the isomorphic repetition of the cosmic pattern on every degree of the scale of being, with the human being as in a particular way the microcosm, a metaphoric encoding of experience through the interplay of resemblances is taken as directly reflecting the structure of reality. Further, it is possible to extrapolate the pattern of resemblances, so as to gain a grasp by analogy of what lies outside our direct understanding. Nevertheless statements such as "Jesus Christ is the Second Adam" or "Jesus Christ is the only Son of God, born of the Father from all eternity" are not taken as optional symbolic statements, which can in principle be replaced by others as equivalent expressions of the underlying religious experience. No, such statements, though metaphorical as based on a play of resemblances, represent and articulate not just the religious experience of a subject but the objective structure and events of the order of reality. All the same, myth need not be taken as an exhaustive account. Much remains unexplained. Reality recedes into mystery. The myth balances and holds together the contradictions we experience rather than solving or removing them. Analogy provides us only with flickering images in the dark. The point, however, still remains: unlike its later critics and defenders, those who live by myth see it as factual not fictional, not as an invented symbolism but as an articulation of things as they are, including the resemblances.

As a comprehensive account, a myth includes an interpretation of human history. To be mythical, an interpretation of history does not have to be cyclical. What makes an account of human history mythical is the relating of the stages and events of human history to the cosmic order. How that is done in the traditional interpretation of Christianity is clearly shown in these two quotations from Christopher Dawson's *Progress and Religion:*

> For Christianity had taught that in Jesus a new principle of divine life had entered the human race and the natural world by which mankind is raised to a higher order. Christ is the head of this restored humanity, the firstborn of the new creation and the life of the Church consists in the progressive extension of the Incarnation by the gradual incorporation of mankind into this higher unity.[23]

Again:

> A new *kind* of life has inserted itself into the cosmic process at a particular point in time under definite historical circumstances and has become the principle of a new order of spiritual progress.[24]

The historical events constituting the Christian order are part of the overall cosmic order, which is realized in stages.

In what I am distinguishing as the mythical interpretation of Christianity, there are not two orders or two worlds, a natural order or world and a supernatural order or world. The mode of interpretation that distinguishes two worlds belongs to what I call the visionary type of Christian religion. In the mythical mode of interpretation, natural and supernatural, profane and sacred, though distinguished as elements, are fitted together into one comprehensive order. The natural or profane is not a world or order but a level in the one world, a world which, though incorporating without destroying the natural, receives its formal determination, its identifying characteristic, from the elevation of humankind and with it the entire cosmos to the supernatural level of participation in the divine life.

Because there is only one order, including natural as well as supernatural elements, the mythical account of that order is given in the form of a realistic narrative, which in an undifferentiated fashion present miracles alongside of ordinary historical events, political actions intermingled with divine interventions.

That narrative is emplotted as a comedy, namely, as a story that ends happily with the harmony of all with all. What is that story?

It is the story of God's love. That love comes first—it originates everything; it remains the support and foundation of everything else; it will bring about the final consummation, when God in God's love will be everything to everyone. In the Christian story God's love goes beyond the gift of creation and the promise of a happiness proportionate to finite human nature. God invites us to a new, personal relation with the divine self. We are God's creatures by nature, dependent upon God, bound to give God grateful service. But God made us for a more intimate union with God. God wanted us to have the kind of personal relation to God that demands the same life, the sharing of the same happiness, with an interchange of love as within a family or between friends. In brief, Christianity is a message about the self-giving of God. Simply by looking at creation we can see that God is a generous giver, giving us many created gifts; but a special message was needed to tell us that God is a tremendous lover who gives God's self to our love. The Christian revelation is the intimate self-disclosure made by God when God called us into personal communion with God's self. That is the meaning of grace and the supernatural order as an elevation of the human race into a participation in the life of God.

But, as the story goes on to relate, because of sin, God's plan could not be a straightforward one. The intimate union with God is not given to isolated individuals but to human beings in community. The original human community was founded upon Adam as the first human being. His rebellion against God put the whole human race in a state of sin, and this sinful situation was reinforced down through human history by an endless repetition of sinful actions. The human race thus fell under the slavery of sin, under the bondage of an external law which became a source of condemnation not of salvation, under the sentence of a meaningless death, and under the power of the Evil One, the Devil. (The Devil, who appears in the Christian story as the enemy of God and of humankind, is the subject of a secondary story concerning the creation and fall of the angels, with the punishment of the wicked angels and the reward of the good angels. The leader of the rebellious, wicked angels becomes the Devil.) How did God remedy the situation and achieve God's original purpose?

He sent his only begotten Son, the preexistent Logos, through whom all things were created, down from heaven to be born of a virgin as a human being. At the Incarnation, God the Son, one with the Father in Godhead, entered the sinful world and submitted himself to conditions of existence that were the result of sin. Entirely free from sin and himself the incarnate Son of God, the man Jesus should by right have had from the outset a glorified human nature in which the Spirit deployed the full effects of the divine life. But he humbled humself and accepted in obedience to his heavenly Father a solidarity with humankind in the condition in which sin had left it. He was made like us in all except sin itself. He became subject to suffering and death. He wanted to overcome sin, suffering, failure and death by his obedient love. His purpose was to transform his solidarity with us in the flesh into a solidarity of glory in the Spirit. "Flesh" here means human beings in their weakness and mortality, in their distance from God. Christ took on the likeness of sinful flesh and became one with us in our wretched state. He then transformed this state in himself and made it possible for us to do the same by being incorporated into him.

By the Resurrection, the reversal of his death and the defeat of the Evil One who brought him to death, Christ entered into a new form of existence. From his glorified humanity there now streams forth the Spirit upon the human race, renewing the face of the earth, beginning with the new community of men and women, the Christian Church, the Body of Christ, the visible embodiment in history and society of the permanent presence of Christ and of his Spirit.

The personal disclosure made by God through Christ revealed to us the Trinity, namely, that God is not one, but three persons: the Father, the Son, and the Holy Spirit. When as Christians we are united to God, we are related to each of these persons. We are brought into their life and share their communion of love. We become children of the Father, able to address God as our Father, related to him in a way comparable to, though far higher than, the way a child is related to its father. That means we are given a likeness to the Son. Our life with the Father is patterned on his. And so it was the Son who became human; we are related to him as his brothers and sisters. Only in Christ, only by being made one with him, do we become children of the Father and share the life of God. Our relation to the Holy Spirit is more difficult to describe.

In the inner mystery of the Trinity, the Holy Spirit comes from Father and Son as their Love, and when as Christians we are united to the Father and Son as their life, the Holy Spirit comes to us as their Gift, the Gift of their Love, the Gift of Love by which they give us themselves. The Spirit dwells within us, assuring us that we are indeed children of the Father and brothers and sisters of Christ. The Spirit keeps us close to them both. Thus we reach personal relations with Father, Son, and Holy Spirit.

That personal communion with the three persons of the Trinity is the reality of our Christian life; it is also the deepest reality of the Church as the redeemed community, the Body of Christ. In its fullness it will be our beatitude, and in its manifestation at the end of history it will be the final glorification and fulfilment of all. It constitutes the essential meaning of the cosmos.

Since the spiritual order of the cosmos cannot be violated with impunity any more than the physical order, those who remain hardened in sin, refusing the demands of God's love, will suffer eternal frustration and pain in hell, thus manifesting in a negative fashion the cosmic plan of God's love.

Such, then, is the mythical version of the Christian story. Like any story, it can be told with incidental variations and with different emphases. In particular, this version may be told in a more historylike fashion, stressing the preparatory actions of God in regard to the Chosen People, prior to the coming of Jesus Christ. I have told it in a manner designed to bring into relief its structure as the representation of a total, cosmic order as normative. It now remains to highlight certain features, so as to facilitate comparison with other versions.

The concept of the Church corresponding to the mythical mode of interpretation is that of a visible institution, the structural elements of which are part of the overall cosmic order and are unchangeable. Just as the mythical view allows one to distinguish various stages in the unfolding of human history, so the visible Church can be seen as existing in various stages of realization, so that one can even speak of the Church from the time of Abel (*Ecclesia ab Abel*), though what is in the forefront is the Church as founded by Jesus Christ upon the apostles. The key characteristic of the Church in the mythical mode of interpretation is that it is an objective institution, like the sacraments prior to human participation, not a product of human creativity but part of the divinely established order of the world and of history. From that standpoint it is inessential whether the institutional order of the Church is understood as an episcopo-papal hierarchy or as a presbyterian order, just as it is inessential to the mythical understanding of society whether its social organization is conceived as monarchical or oligarchical. The decisive point is whether the Church is an objective structure, given as part of an order prior to human participation, or a changing product of human activity.

The second feature to underline is that in this conception the essential vehicle or bearer of religious knowledge and value in the world is not the individual but the Church as a cultural community endowed with a magisterial authority. Hence the stress laid upon tradition, which is the extension of the Church's teaching over time and space. Myth of its nature is exclusive and coercive, because it is a social charter that articulates an objective order, independent of human volition. There is no room for a pluralism that allows equal validity to other accounts of reality, and toleration can be only a patience with the weakness and ignorance of individuals, incidental to the maintenance of the one true order, permissible provided it does not threaten its stability. The mythical order and the doctrines that formulate its elements have a permanent and unchanging truth. Society can ignore this only at its peril, and dissident elements must be eliminated from the body of society, just as disease must be removed from the physical body.

One can see how the stress upon the Church and tradition favors an organicist mode of argumentation. The Church, tradition, the cosmos itself are conceived after the manner of an organism; their development as an organic process. Individual parts and events are related to the whole and made subordinate to its finality. An outstanding example of the organicist mode of argumentation as applied to the Christian fact is Newman's *An Essay on the Development of Christian Doctrine.*

In the context of the Christian religion as myth, namely, as the comprehensive account of the one order of reality, an account revealed by God and accepted by faith, the function of human intelligence is seen as *faith seeking understanding,* namely, as the analysis, formulation, and defense of elements of the myth as doctrines. Thus the mythical interpretation of Christianity corresponds to the doctrinal or dogmatic mode of interpretation. The work of human intelligence directly concerning the myth is subject to the authority of revelation, which in practice means to the control of its official guardians. Further, the work of human intelligence concerning the natural elements of the world order comes indirectly under the authority of revelation and the control of the guardians of revelation, both because there is only one total cosmic and historical order into which the natural elements within the grasp of human reason have to be fitted and because in that order as traditionally understood by Christians human reason has been corrupted or at least weakened by sin and needs God's healing grace (*gratia sanans*) for its natural functioning.

The third feature is that the predominant practical expressions of the mythical interpretation of Christianity is ritual. The sacraments are given a place of honor and the teaching on their *ex opere operato* efficacy removes their saving power from dependence upon the personal holiness of the minister and, though minimal conditions are required for their fruitfulness, from dependence upon the merits of the recipient. In brief, there is set up an objective scheme of salvation, which is related to the cosmic order. In the course of Christian history, the objective scheme received much secondary elaboration in the proliferation of external practice such as pilgrimages, worship of relics, penances of various descriptions, and so on. The details are unimportant. What is important is the attitude according to which the practice of religion consisted in the performance of external procedures related to an objective scheme the efficacy of which was essentially independent of the persons carrying out the procedures, even though a minimum of personal dispositions was a condition for fruitful participation in the working of the scheme.

In its conception of a normative order as prior to human intelligence and creativity, in its stress upon tradition and the Church as indispensable bearers of revealed knowledge and value, and in its view of language as no mere external tool but as reflecting the patterning of reality, the mythical type of Christian religion is inevitably conservative in its attitude to social reality and history. Nevertheless there are different kinds of conservatism, which should not be exclusively identified with a reactive rigidity.

I conclude this account of the first type of Christian religion with some brief historical remarks to relate it to the concrete Christian tradition. The full emergence of this type had to await the integration of Christianity into the Roman world. The eschatological thrust of the original Christian message, which corresponds to the visionary type, was blunted, and the Christian scheme of salvation was built into a cosmic order. This then became the foundation for the religio-political system of the Middle Ages—or, rather, systems, because the church-state relationship took a different shape in the Byzantine Empire from that in the West. Paradoxically the greater independence, indeed the dominance, achieved by the Church under the papacy in the West germinated a process of secularization in response. Already in the Middle Ages themselves, the total order of Western Christendom began to crack. What was later called secularization got away to an early start. In the present context secularization is the disengagement of various areas of society from subordination to the myth and its guardians. The Reformation and religious wars by breaking up the unity of Christendom facilitated the process. The Enlightenment explored the intellectual and political alternatives to the Christian myth. Despite the partially successful attempts to restore the old order after it, the French Revolution may rightly be seen as marking the end of Christendom. Nevertheless the struggle both political and intellectual, between upholders of the myth and modern unbelievers continued down through the nineteenth century, to result in the present century in the situation where there is a lack of any effective relationship between the Christian faith and modern society. But what happened to the myth itself in this process?

There took place a deformation and hardening of the myth into dead doctrines by its severance from its experiential base. Even granted the conviction of those who live by the myth that it is not a record of variable subjective experience but an objective account of the order of reality, it still depends for its meaningfulness on its ability to offer a satisfactory interpretation of our experience of the world and of God. If the connection is lost between the mythical themes of sin, grace, redemption and the experience of the conditions of human existence, namely, guilt, failure, suffering, and death, the myth becomes a body of doctrine to be believed but with no power to transform human living. If the mythical talk of God and of our personal communion with God becomes severed from the experience of the mysterious, transcendent presence hidden in the nothingness that surrounds finite human existence, the myth becomes a dogma coming from outside our lives and describing a realm in which we profess our belief but which is utterly remote from the actual reality of our lives. And that is what happened. From the latter part of the Middle Ages down through into the present, the living Christian myth was petrified into a dead deposit of reified doctrines to be defended *pro aris et focis* against unbelievers. As the modern world moved increasingly away from the previous Christian order, the link between ordinary human existence in this world and the Christian myth became more and more tenuous. Even the worlds of science fiction now have a stronger accent of reality.

The doctrinalized form of the Christian myth reached its apogee in the textbooks that dominated the Catholic theological scene from the eighteenth century until the Second Vatican Council. It is only fair to add, however, that the tradition of Catholic spirituality continued to make the mythico-doctrinal presentation of Christian faith a source of life. I am thinking of such books as Abbot Marmion's *Christ in His Mysteries*[25], from which during my student days many of us seminarians drew our spiritual nourishment amid the aridities of textbook theology. That spiritual tradition led into the catechetical revival, which again tried to bring life back into Christian doctrine.

All the same, the content of the Christian myth in the form of a set of reified doctrines was fiercely defended point by point, in a literalistic interpretation, by individuals and groups who found their sense of security and identity threatened by the revolutionary changes in European society during and after the French Revolution. The mythical type of Christian religion in some such deformed version is what we find in Protestant neoconfessionalists and Catholic traditionalists and ultramontanists of the nineteenth century and in the various fundamentalist groups and movements of the nineteenth and twentieth, though some of the latter proclaim a visionary version of Christian religion.

At this point let me elaborate a distinction between two different kinds of conservative. First, there are those I have just been referring to, who in a political context are restorationists and reactionaries, rejecting the Enlightenment and the French Revolution and working to restore the status quo ante and who in a religious context are traditionalists and fundamentalists, regarding revelation and tradition as a fixed, unchanging body of truths and rejecting all change and pluralism. Second, there is the conservatism that arose as a response within the Enlightenment, correcting its one-sidedness and endeavouring to reconcile its critical rationality with a retention of the substance of tradition. In a political context that conservative outlook is represented by thinkers such as Burke, Coleridge, and Acton. Their method of argument was not just an appeal to authority but broadly empirical, insofar as they considered it appropriate to argue from human experience and to ascertain the facts, historical and experiential, in dealing with the validity of social, ethical, and religious claims. The result was a concept of tradition as cumulative experience, subject therefore to change whether as development or as decline, which distinguished them as conservative, from reactionaries, who did not acknowledge history and development. In a religious context the conservatives in the second sense were those who saw tradition as a dynamic process rather than as a static deposit. Those nineteenth-century thinkers we usually call religious liberals belonged to a conservative tradition of discourse, accepting a prior order as normative but interpreting it as open to development. I have in mind Drey, Möhler and the Tübingen School, Schleiermacher and the other Reformed theologians dealt with so admirably by Brian Gerrish in *Tradition and the Modern World: Reformed Theology in the Nineteenth Century*.[26] With those we may group the English thinkers Coleridge, Newman, Maurice, and Thomas Arnold. All these thinkers differ widely from one another on particular issues; and yet each of them, as Gerrish remarks concerning those he treats, "illuminates the place of tradition in the modern world."[27] Although they were more often than not suspected of heterodoxy by traditionalists and fundamentalists, they all deeply respected tradition and moved it forward in a positive fashion to meet the new questions of modernity. They were, however, conservatives in their fundamental presupposition concerning the priority of a normative order and differ in that respect from liberals properly so-called. For that reason, Newman spent his life opposing liberalism in religion.

The Catholic theology that found official expression at the Second Vatican Council is fundamentally conservative and represents an attempted continuance of the mythical version of the Christian religion. The question arises whether the myth can live much longer. Are we not in a situation that cannot be met by an orderly development of traditional categories, but which demands something radically new? How far, for instance, does the myth in its present form, however flexibly interpreted, enable us (1) to live without dissembling in the context of nuclear terror, (2) to meet from our position of privilege the social and political demands of the oppressed majority of humankind, (3) to face the coming desuetude of most of our social institutions through the impact of high technology, and (4) to welcome positively the active pluralism of religions in the global community? A myth must relate to the deepest challenges posed by human existence in this world if it is to live as myth and not survive merely as a piece of folklore.

CHAPTER 4

Second Model: Pragmatic Christianity

The pragmatic version of the Christian religion is derivative in relation to the first. It presupposes that the Christian myth has ceased to operate as an overarching totality but has been reduced to its elements. These elements are still taken seriously, and for that reason we are dealing with a version of Christianity, not with a secular humanism; but they are subject to critical examination, and the criterion for their interpretation and assessment is their relationship to human moral striving. The focus is no longer upon an objective cosmic order but upon the human struggle for righteousness. The Christian religion is essentially a practical way of life.

Three closely related cultural changes form the background for the emergence of the pragmatic type of Christian religion.

The first was the shift from a cosmocentric to an anthropocentric outlook. This was a feature of the Renaissance, and it was shared by the Christian humanists, such as Erasmus. Although there was no denial of Christian doctrine and ritual, the plea for a return to evangelical simplicity meant that the Christian religion was not seen primarily as an objective system of salvation, complementing the order of the cosmos, but as a personal relationship with God, manifesting itself in a way of life based upon the double commandment of love. That was followed by the second cultural shift: the focusing upon the mind and mental processes, the highlighting of consciousness, and the division between conscious states as events in an inner life and events in an external world.[28] To grasp the change here, it should be noted that, while the body-mind distinction was known to the Greeks and medievals, the processes of sense perception were put, prior to Descartes, on the side of the body. Descartes, however, used "thought" (*cogitatio, pensée*) to cover imagining and feeling as well as doubting, understanding, affirming, denying, willing, and refusing: in short, "thought" referred to all conscious states. In that way, Descartes established the mind as a separate entity, the seat of consciousness or mental processes, the thing which thinks, over against the body, constituted by extension and understood in purely mechanical terms with the rest of the material universe. His dichotomy between mind and body implied a denial of the historical character of thought and a leaving behind of the temporal world of lived human experience. To quote Levi:

> . . . the *real process* of thinking disappears, along with its historical grounding and dialectical movement, and we are left with a consciousness *überhaupt,* impersonal and static, cut off from historicity, past time, and memory, a pure mental act and center constituting the scientific observer, as clear and transparent a medium as a reflecting pool or the lens of a microscope.[29]

Thus for Descartes the existence of consciousness was the first principle, from which the other features of his system were deduced. Although Locke's empiricism was opposed to Descartes's rationalism, Locke too assimilated the sensory and the intellectual, so that the mind-body distinction fell not between reason and the living, sensate body but between consciousness and what is not consciousness. Locke's theory of knowledge was based upon the investigation of mental processes. He brought into relief a new use, derived from Descartes, of the word "idea" for the content of any conscious act, namely, for any immediate object, whether sensory or intellectual, of the thinking mind. Knowledge took place in an inner space, in which ideas as representations of external realities are scrutinized for signs of their accuracy.

The story continues with Kant's attempt to make epistemology the foundational discipline, insofar as it determined the limits and conditions of possibility of all knowing, thus grounding and legitimizing other disciplines and culture generally. Kant still worked within the supposition of the mind as inner space, containing the elements and processes required for knowledge. His knowing subject did not have a full historical reality. Hence the subsequent turn to the concrete reality of the historical subject in Hegel, Kierkegaard, Nietzsche, Heidegger, Buber, and others. But my concern at the moment is with the earlier highlighting of consciousness as an inner world, set apart from the outer world of external events.

The result religiously was a new pressure for the internalization of Christian religion. To say this is not inconsistent with the identification previously made of the pragmatic type of Christian religion now under review with a practical way of life. Practice in this type of religion is no longer conformity to an objective system but fully personal, moral action, rooted in the explicit belief and conscious commitment of the individual. Internalization was negatively the downgrading of ritual and of rituallike external practices. These were seen as encouraging a magical rather than a moral understanding of religion. In opposition to them, there was, positively, an insistence that the practice of religion must be responsible, personal performance, with an engagement that demands the full consciousness of the human spirit. No one could rely upon the working of an objective system to make up for the inadequacy of personal response. According to the moral mode of interpreting Christianity, nothing could ever replace even in part one's personal response, the depth and sincerity of which is the measure of one's Christian life. There was no sense of being carried along by tradition or of living in the supportive context of a prior order, authoritatively interpreted.

The internalization of religion I have been describing does not make religion a purely subjective secret of the heart. Religion is not identified with some distinctive interior experience or mystical intuition. Far from being immediately experienced or intuitively known, God is merely posited as a moral or intellectual need. Religion is effective moral practice and involves Christians in the task of building a community based upon love and establishing justice and peace upon earth. The personal religious commitment of individuals relates them socially in their moral striving and pursuit of righteousness.

Where this type of religion reflects the new prominence of consciousness as an inner world and stands in contrast to the mythical type is in its turning inward to find ineluctable truth, not outward to some external rule of faith or magisterial authority. Epistemology in the form of apologetics becomes the foundational discipline for religion as well as for science. Further, the inner world also becomes foundational inasmuch as the basis of morality is no longer conformity to a prior order but in the disposition and intention of the subject. Conscience becomes supreme.

Philosophically, then, consciousness became an inner arena in which inherited or previously acquired elements were tested and either given certitude or purged from the mind. That philosophic search for an inner ground came about during the same period in which pastoral movements, issuing from both the Reformation and Counter-Reformation, were trying to bring the ordinary people of Europe to a truly personal faith and committed religious practice. At the time, both political and ecclesiastical authorities were demanding a greater degree of personal adherence to whatever they regarded as the authentic form of Christianity than had ever been demanded previously. One must do more than conform; one must personally believe and devoutly perform. There was also a sustained attempt to root out not only heresy but also all those folk beliefs and practices considered as tainted with magic, superstition, and traces of paganism. That pastoral effort differed greatly from the philosophical quest for inward certitude. The philosophers skirted scepticism and retained only those traditional elements that met their criteria. The religious preachers tried to make people internalize the whole traditional body of beliefs and practices. But both were concerned in a way that was culturally new with mental processes and engaged in a battle for the mind, seeking to ground knowledge or faith in the inner world of consciousness. The religious reformers who aimed at bringing the multitude to a truly personal faith, instead of a vicarious sharing in a system sustained by religious specialists—priests, monks, nuns, saints—unwittingly took part in the dissolution of the Christian myth and its replacement by an individually grounded way of life.

This brings me to the third cultural shift: the change—in Timothy Reiss's terms—from a discourse of patterning to an analytico-referential form of discourse.

The discourse of patterning served to place the user in a context. It articulated relationships within a total order. The user of the discourse, the things brought to expression, and the images and words used in the utterance were all within the same overarching whole. Discourse was not an instrument of power, enabling an external knower to master and manipulate things from outside themselves. It was the uncovering of the pattern of internal relationships within an all-embracing order, with a consequent shift in the stress or shading laid upon particular elements and relations. That was, in brief, the mythical tradition of discourse.

In the seventeenth century there was a transition from such a discourse of patterning to an analytico-referential mode of discourse. The transition may be described as "a passage from what one might call a discursive *exchange within* the world to the expression of knowledge as a reasoning practice upon the world".[30] It puts a subject over against an object, with a mediating sign system in between. "Its exemplary formal statement is *cogito-ergo-sum* (reason—semiotic mediating system—world), but it is found no less in the new discursive 'instauration' worked out by Bacon. . . ."[31] The effort to comprehend by placing signs and things into a pattern of resemblances was replaced by the effort to make things usable.[32]

The world, therefore, is now regarded as a fixed object of analysis, quite distinct from the words, images, and forms of discourse by which it is represented and spoken of. Words and images are no longer understood as in some way inherent in the object or essential to it. Language becomes an arbitrary, formal system of signs, but precisely as such it can be organized so as to analyse and represent the structure of the world. Language, therefore, as an order of signs coincides on the one side with the logical order of reason and on the other side with the structural organization of the world. Consequently the use of language in a process of accumulating details gives us the object referentially and in so doing analyzes its structure.

The impact upon the status of religious belief of the change in the form of discourse went deep. The aim now of any discourse with a claim to intellectual rigour was complete clarity and logical accuracy of meaning and reference. Metaphor was regarded as rhetorical ornament, and any measure of meaning symbolic language might have could be translated into literal statements. Discourse no longer used analogy or conveyed meaning by the patterning of resemblances. But religious language depended upon analogy and the use of resemblances, because the transcendence of its objects put them beyond direct apprehension and structural analysis by the human mind. Hence the link between religious belief and reason became weakened where it was not destroyed. Statements of religious belief seemed to lack rigour and adequate grounding as theoretical statements. Consequently the Christian religion was defended chiefly as a practical way of life, its language primarily concerned with moral imperatives, values, and ideals, embodied in part in examples and stories. Any strictly theoretical statements either became postulates of its moral demands or were reduced, with the supernatural elements eliminated, to a handful of truths that could plausibly claim to be inferences of natural reason.

To recapitulate: The pragmatic version of Christianity arose when the Christian religion ceased to function mythically as an overarching totality or taken-for-granted whole. The mythical elements in the form of doctrines and rites persisted, linked to one another loosely or closely. These elements were however subject to testing and appraisal before the tribunal of consciousness, where the standards of an analytico-referential discourse were dominant. The context was unfavorable to speculative religious thought. The emphasis therefore shifted to Christianity as a practical way of life or ethical system. This is still conceived in religious terms, such as the fatherhood of God and the brotherhood of God's children, the kingdom of righteousness, the double commandment of love, the community of the just, and so on. But all these expressions are different ways of formulating the moral imperatives governing human existence. Theoretical affirmations are admitted only insofar as they are in some way required or bound up with the ethical character of human life. But what in this context becomes of the Christian story?

The first point to notice in answer is that within the pragmatic version of Christian religion the narrative character of Christian teaching was largely lost sight of. Interpretation did not dwell upon the unity, shape, or dramatic sequence of the account of God's dealings with the human race through Jesus Christ. Jesus was seen as the supreme teacher and exemplar. His words were to be studied and followed; his example was the object of meditation and imitation. His clear commands and unsullied actions opened a sure path to morality for human beings confused and darkened by their sins and failures. He taught a righteousness based upon love, not confined to external observances, but rooted interiorly in a loving heart; and he himself was the personal realization of that higher righteousness.[33] But the specifically Christian meanings lay not in his life as a story but in the content of his teaching and in the moral goodness of all his actions.

The lack of a sense of narrative explains the change, studied by Hans Frei in *The Eclipse of Biblical Narrative,*[34] in the evaluation of the biblical stories. The appreciation of them as historylike was distorted by an exclusive concern with their historical truth at the expense of their narrative meaning. According to Frei, the biblical stories are realistic or historylike narratives. They are historylike in the identity of their meaning with the story as told, but that meaning did not depend upon the story's being an empirically accurate report of events as they actually occurred, namely, upon their being historical in the modern sense. From the eighteenth century onwards, the two categories, history and historylike were confused. "But in effect, the realistic or historylike quality of biblical narratives, acknowledged by all, instead of being examined for the bearing it had in its own right on meaning and interpretation was immediately transposed into the quite different issue of whether or not the realistic narrative was historical."[35] In other words, the biblical texts are realistic narratives, resulting from a fusion of history and fiction. Their point is missed and their meaning lost if they are interpreted as straight history. As far as the meaning they are intended to convey is concerned, a meaning embodied in the story as story, it does not matter whether they recount history or not, reliably or not. It is enough that they are historylike as realistic narratives in the identity of what is represented or meant with the representation or meaning as articulated in the words of the text. The use of biblical texts to reconstruct events as they actually occurred in the world outside the texts does not belong to the meaning they have in their own right as texts. But from the eighteenth century onward, the biblical narratives were not considered as narratives or the biblical story as a story. The texts were data to be used to establish what actually happened. How far that enterprise was or could be successful does not concern us here. The present point is simply to note the weakening in Christian thought and living of the impact of the Christian story as a story.

When, however, the Christian story as a story was told in the pragmatic version of Christian religion, the tendency was to emplot it as a tragedy. The death of Jesus Christ was at the center as a supreme instance of the conflict found in human existence between virtue and fortune, between morality and success or happiness. The good man, despite his goodness, meets with opposition and rejection. He is misunderstood. Far from being rewarded for the good that he brings and teaches, he rouses enmity, and the return he must expect is suffering and even death at the hands of those he has loved and served. Human existence is essentially tragic inasmuch as those who oppose the good know not what they do but are themselves victims of circumstance, caught in ignorance and prejudice, fear, and inhibitions, for which they are not fully responsible. Human conflict is a night battle where the identity of friend and foe are lost in confusion. Human existence is tragic, because the finite conditions within which it is lived out make it impossible to resolve all oppositions, so as to establish harmony. The human story is not a straightforward struggle between good and evil, summoning us to heroic courage, but a confused conflict between good and good, calling us to a patient resignation to our finitude. The crucifixion and the cross as a permanent symbol teach us not to expect our virtue to be rewarded with earthly success and happiness. After centuries of preparation, Jesus Christ himself was tragically misunderstood and rejected by the Chosen People.

In the pragmatic version of the Christian religion, the tragic reading of the story of Jesus Christ was not cancelled by belief in the resurrection, because that belief had become problematic. There was a general tendency to reduce or even to eliminate the miraculous element in Christianity. Where miracles were kept, they were seen as proofs of the divine origin of the Christian message—reduced to a moral message—rather than as the manifestation of the presence of a higher, supernatural level of human existence. Hence the resurrection, where retained as a reality, was understood as an outstanding proof of Christ's teaching, rather than as a transformation of human life, a transformation in which we all are to participate. Further, the reading of the biblical texts as straight history created a difficulty about the historical character of the resurrection as an event. How could the resurrection be interpreted as an historical happening? Its supernatural character seemed to remove it from history as ordinarily understood. But if it was not historical, how should we interpret it?

Thus the difficulties surrounding the resurrection in a culture dominated by the analytico-referential mode of discourse prevented it from functioning as the governing event in the Christian story. The resurrection was relegated to apologetics, and the Christian story was given its climax in the crucifixion as the tragic death of a righteous man.

What, now, is the concept of the Church corresponding to the pragmatic mode of interpreting the Christian religion? A preliminary remark is in order. Pragmatic Christianity is anticonfessional and pluralist in its orientation. Because doctrinal differences are not regarded as of first importance, such differences are not considered as justifying exclusive divisions among Christians. Religion is emphatically identified with moral practice, not with the acceptance of a set of beliefs—even the devils may believe in the doctrinal sense. Against the background of a divided Christian Church and of warring confessional groups, the moral mode of interpreting Christianity insists upon toleration and pluralism. Christians should lay aside their disputes about doctrine and cooperate in bringing about the practical embodiment in society of Christian values.

In the context of that general attitude, the key principle governing the conception of the Church is the distinction between Christendom or the Christian world and the visible Christian Churches as institutions. There is a refusal to regard the Churches, either singly or together, as exhausting the presence of Christianity in the world. Trutz Rendtorff sees the defining characteristic of the modern, post-Enlightenment religious situation as being the emigration of Christian values outside of the Churches.[36]

To put it in another way, pragmatic Christianity represents an attempt to refashion the Church so that it no longer stood on the side of the State as an institution of power, but belonged as a social system to the bourgeois public sphere, which was grounded upon the principle of freedom and mutual exchange. In the analysis of Habermas,[37] the bourgeois public sphere is the sphere of private people formed into a public. There was a polarization of State on the one hand and society on the other. There developed the basically privatized but publicly relevant sphere of commerce and social work. That public sphere made the claim over against the governmentally ruled public sphere that the latter should deal with it concerning the basically free or privatized affairs of business and public opinion. The corresponding concept of the Church was that of a voluntary association in the public sphere, namely, a basically private organization, built upon free independent enquiry and decision but with a publicly relevant function, that of the ethical education of society. The Churches as visible institutions were regarded as subordinate to the Christian world. They were schools of Christianity; but the school is not the whole of life, and alongside the official Christianity of the Churches is the free, autonomous Christianity of mature, adult Christians.

It follows that in the pragmatic version of Christian religion, the essential vehicle or bearer of religious knowledge and value is the individual, not however in isolation but in association with other like-minded individuals. The social dimension of religion is not denied; indeed, in many respects it is insisted upon because of the moral orientation of this type of Christianity. What, however, is rejected is the claim of any priestly caste to impose its will upon other Christians and to insist upon unquestioning obedience. This is seen as an heteronomy, violating the freedom and responsibility of the individual. The social forms of the Christian religion are, it is held, created from below, not imposed from above.

In the context of emphasis upon moral practice and the responsibility of the individual, the function of reason in the pragmatic kind of Christianity is predominantly critical and reductionistic. It is the exercise of critical rationality that dissolves the exclusive claims made by the different confessions and prevents the free, responsible individual from falling into the heteronomy of confessionalism. The moral mode of interpretation introduces a good dose of doctrinal scepticism. One can also say it favors a mechanistic mode of discourse, insofar it seeks out the laws governing religious phenomena, puts forward causal explanations and analyzes the different functions and relationships of the variety of particular religious elements.

It is well to note that the emphasis upon critical reason has a positive, not just a negative basis. Reason in its critical function is seen as the principle of nonviolent communication among men and women. It is also understood as a democratic principle, calling upon each person individually to sift questions. There is a contrast here between speculative reason as originating worldviews and metaphysical systems and critical reason. Speculative reason is regarded as an elitist principle, being usually the attribute of an educated and specialist group. Critical reason is the function of every person, who should freely and responsibly participate in the ongoing discourse of the public sphere.

In view of the description already given, it hardly needs saying that the predominant practical expression of the pragmatic interpretation of Christianity is moral action in this world. Put it in this way: it clearly belongs to the Life and Work, rather than to the Faith and Order stream of the Ecumenical Movement.

Ideologically it is liberal in its attitude to social reality and history. Liberalism, it will be recalled, as an ideology assumes a plurality of orders, existing in mutual toleration because grounded practically not theoretically. What that assumption might lead to in the religious sphere may be seen, by way of example, in considering Newman's opposition to liberal religion. It was a lifelong opposition. In the speech delivered upon his becoming a cardinal, he said, "Thirty, forty, fifty years I have resisted to the best of my powers the spirit of Liberalism in religion."[38] Yearley constructs the type of religion Newman had in mind by outlining what Newman saw as the first principles of liberal religion, forming its religious outlook:

> There are six such principles: (1) human nature is good; (2) private judgment is obligatory; (3) deity is a principle discoverable through examination of evidence; (4) revelation is a manifestation not a mystery; (5) useful goods are primary; and (6) education is salvatory. The first pair reflects its general vision of humanity, the second pair its view of deity and the world's relation to deity. The final pair focuses on the new "salvatory" social matrix that can fulfill humanity.[39]

What Newman rejects in his denial of the third principle is that religious truth is open to all without a preparation of the heart. The sixth principle expresses the liberal idea that education can fully actualize people.

Newman is often thought of as a liberal, chiefly because of his recognition of the necessity and function of an educated laity in the Church, in contrast to the narrow clericalism and authoritarianism of the contemporary Roman Church—which was indeed a liberal stance. His idea of development also gave him a view of tradition as a dynamic process rather than as a static deposit. But Newman's concept of language, of reason, of tradition, of community, of a prior normative order places him in the conservative tradition.

I conclude now this sketch of pragmatic Christianity with some brief historical remarks.

Enno Van Gelder in his book *The Two Reformations* contends that the "major Reformation" was not the Protestant movement of the sixteenth century but Christian humanism, which had its origin in Italy in the fifteenth century and was spread over the whole of Europe by the sixteenth century. He considers Christian humanism the major Reformation because it was a revolutionary shift in the understanding of the Christian religion, a radical change of outlook, which was a far greater factor than the Protestant Reformation in the development of modern culture. The change was in effect the emergence of what I have called pragmatic Christianity. Some of the representatives of the major Reformation were Catholics, some were Protestant. They did not openly deny the official tenets of the Churches to which they belonged. But in their interpretation the Christian religion became not so much a religion of salvation as a philosophy of life, the chief practices of religion not communal rites or sacraments but individual moral action, and the guiding standard less official teaching than reason.

The great popularizer of the major Reformation was Erasmus, though he was not himself a very original thinker, philosophically or theologically. His works, however, were read by laity and priests more than those of anyone else. The Arminian-Socinian movement then carried Erasmian ideas into the latter part of the sixteenth century and beyond. Trevor-Roper maintains that the Arminian-Socinian movement is not an extension of Calvinism, as is often supposed, but an independent movement, with a distinct origin and a continuous tradition. Its distinctive ideas preceded Calvinism as Erasmus preceded Calvin, though it was at times subsumed into Calvinism and became a solvent force within it.[41]

One can continue and in that fashion trace the tradition of humanist, antidogmatic, liberal, rationalist Christianity from Erasmus to the present day. Friedrich Heer does so in his large volume on the Third Force, *Die Dritte Kraft*.[42] Some of the people who would figure in any such account would be Locke and the Deists; Voltaire, in many respects the Erasmus of the eighteenth century; Lessing and Kant; Semler (1725–91), the founder of Protestant liberal theology, with his "free mode of doctrine" (*freie Lehrart*); his followers, Tzschirner (1778–1828) and Bretschneider (1776–1848), with their ethical rationalism; Ritschl (1822–1889) and the Ritschlians, especially Adolf von Harnack, whose *What is Christianity?* (1900) may be taken as the classic example of what I have called pragmatic Christianity.

What renders difficult the discernment of the line of pragmatic Christianity in the nineteenth century is the Romantic response to the Enlightenment and the development of a conservative tradition, distinct on the one hand from the reactionary, anti-Enlightenment tradition and on the other hand from the rationalist, antisupernaturalist, liberal tradition. As I have already remarked, some of those in the nineteenth century we think of as religious liberals—as, for example, Schleiermacher and Newman—belong to the conservative tradition rather than to that of liberal rationalism or, in other words, that of the pragmatic ethical version of Christian religion.

The distinction comes across very clearly if one reads *Christianity at the Cross-Roads,* the last book of the Modernist George Tyrrell. In it he deplores the fact that Modernism is confused by both friend and foe with Liberal Protestantism as exemplified in Harnack's *What is Christianity?* That confusion is to forget that Loisy's *L'Evangile et l'Eglise* was directed precisely against the Liberal Protestantism of Harnack. Modernism for Tyrrell keeps the transcendence that Harnack surrenders. He goes on to distinguish Modernism from orthodoxy, both in its old form, which insists upon the immutability of doctrine, and in the new version, which allows a merely dialectical development. The Modernists in contrast take over Newman's principle of organic development, but, unlike Newman, they do not use it in the service of a dogmatic Christianity but regard as inevitable a critical reassessment of the fundamental categories of Catholic Christianity. The Modernist, according to Tyrrell,

> thinks that the Catholic Christian Idea contains, within itself, the power continually to revise its categories, and to shape its embodiment to its growth, and that such a transformation or revolution would be within the orderly process of its life—merely a step forward to a fuller and better self-consciousness from a confused and instinctive self-consciousness.[44]

That to me is a statement of a conservative reinterpretation of the mythical type of Christianity, not an instance of the pragmatic type of Christian religion. The pragmatic version is represented better—this time within the context of analytical philosophy—by Braithwaite's famous essay, "An Empiricist's View of the Nature of Religious Belief."[45] For Braithwaite the primary use of religious assertions is to announce allegiance to a set of moral principles. In the case of the Christian religion, that allegiance is to an agapeistic way of life. The intention to pursue the Christian way of life is, however, associated with a particular set of stories. Consequently we may conclude, "To assert the whole set of assertions of the Christian religion is both to tell the Christian doctrinal story and to confess allegiance to the Christian way of life."[46] There you have in Braithwaite, it seems to me, an excellent example of an up-to-date version of the second model of Christian religion, the pragmatic.

CHAPTER 5

Third Model: Visionary Christianity

Neither the mythical nor the pragmatic type of Christian religion is able fully to meet the needs of the oppressed and marginal elements in human society for deliverance and integration. Although the mythical version's concept of a prior normative order can serve as a critical principle in reforming an existing state of affairs, the insistence upon totality tends to legitimate actual institutions and the order they embody and thus exclude any radical critique of the present and any radical hope for a different future. The pragmatic type in its turn is both elitist and gradualist in its focus upon human moral action and in its reliance upon reason. It expresses the attitude of those who because of their wealth and their position in society have a sense of power as moral agents; it does not appeal to those who are crushed by a sense of powerlessness. Further, the stress upon rational, moral agency leads pragmatic Christians to shun revolutionary solutions and to urge instead evolutionary reforms. That, however, does not meet the intense desire for deliverance and the demand for an immediancy of salvation found among the common people during periods of upheaval and change.

Hence, when a mythical order breaks up and a dominant myth loses its taken-for-granted character and ceases in a period of disruption and transition adequately to encode the now intense and violent experience and hopes of the multitude, a visionary form of religion comes into existence. It flourishes alongside the pragmatic, which serves as the refuge of an educated minority.

The defining characteristic of the visionary type of religion is the distinction between two worlds: the present world of sin and corruption, destined for destruction, and the future world of salvation, hidden at present and still to be made manifest. Sometimes the weight falls upon the destruction of the old, sometimes upon the coming of the new. In the mild variety of visionary religion, all the attention is on the emergence of the new, so that the destruction of the old is simply its passing away when the new comes. In the violent, revolutionary variety, the intense belief and desire that the existing order should be destroyed as evil eclipses the thought of what might be the new. There is also another range of variation in the visionary type, according to whether the accent falls upon the social, external, cosmic dimension of the drama or upon its individual, inward form. At one extreme there is an existentialist version, where the concern is with the individual decision by which a person in a conversion renounces the forces of darkness and adheres to the light. At the other extreme, the apocalyptic focus upon the cosmic battle results in an indifference to the fate of the individual. But whatever the variations, this type of religion is dominated by a dualism of two worlds and the conflict between them. It is that dualism that distinguishes even the individualist variety from the mystical type of religion, where the visible world is left behind as unreal but not as evil. Another contrast with the mystical type is that the visionary type looks for the radically new, whereas the mystical type uncovers what is a permanent, present reality behind appearances.

The Christian religion originated as a visionary form of religion against the background of the breakup of both the Jewish and the Hellenistic mythical worlds. At the time of Christ, both Judaism and Hellenism were in a fluid state. There was a proliferation of movements and groups, without any taken-for-granted, overarching religious order. The immediate context for the Christian message or *kerygma* was the apocalyptic expectation of the irruption of a new order and the destruction of the old. The coming order was seen not as rising out of the present but as breaking into the present by an act of God. Apocalyptic hope was a hope for the radically new, and this took the form of an imminent expectation. The new order was upon us and would be manifested at any moment. Such was the hope of the first Christians, for whom the resurrection of Christ was the advent of the final Kingdom shortly to be manifested in its full glory and cosmic consummation. There was indeed a variety of stresses, as the New Testament itself documents. Existentialist commentators highlight the *kerygma* as a summons to an individual decision here and now. Others underline the elements traditionally associated with apocalyptic, such as the cosmic conflict, the destruction of empires and the events of the end of history. Under each variety, however, lies the intensity of a desire for an immediate salvation that constitutes the source of the visionary type of religion.

The Christian story in the visionary type of Christianity is centered upon the death and resurrection of Jesus and is emplotted as a romance, in which Jesus is the victorious hero, successfully completing his quest and overcoming the forces of evil. It is told in some such fashion as this: Jesus came into our sinful world and accepted freely the conditions of our sinful existence. As our leader, he began the difficult and painful journey back to the Father. He came into conflict with the Devil and with the forces of evil, both angelic and human. These eventually brought him to the Cross. But the free and obedient love with which he accepted his death transformed apparent defeat into victory. It changed his death into a sacrifice, a symbol or expression of that surrender by which human beings enter into union with God. By his resurrection, the outcome of his death, Jesus reached the end of his journey back to the Father, gained the decisive victory over the Devil and the powers of darkness and entered upon his lordship as the glorified hero. In his risen humanity he guides human beings by the Spirit, enabling them to follow in his footsteps, complete their journey or quest, and share in his victory. That is the essential core of the story. The cosmic conflict of the apocalyptic literature is the death and resurrection of Christ writ large and presented in all its ramifications in history and nature.

The concept of the Church according to this version of Christian religion is that of the visible group or sect as a contingent, partial embodiment of the invisible community of the elect or predestined. The Christian Church is not, then, an institution to be integrated into the social and political order or to be developed as an organization with its own structure and laws. The true Church is the invisible community of the saints to be revealed when this present world is overthrown and the new world made manifest. Meanwhile, those to whom the vision of the end has been revealed gather together in their common expectation and help one to live withdrawn from this world destined for destruction.

Consequently, the bearer of religious knowledge and value in visionary Christianity is neither the Churches as institutions integrated into present society nor the autonomous individual, but the community of the elect or true believers, the destined remnant. There is no place for an explicit acknowledgment of the creative work of human intelligence or the critical function of reason. As the word "apocalypse," which is Greek for revelation, indicates, the contention on which the visionary type rests is that God through visions and revelations has made known God's hidden plan. All the same, despite the claim to the authority of a divine revelation, visionary religion in fact involves a considerable activity of reason and imagination in elaborating the symbolism of the end of this order and of the new order to come. The mode of argumentation is predominantly formist, inasmuch as the concern is with individual symbols, rather than upon a mythical whole. Elements of this visible world are chosen as revelatory symbols of the world to come. The work here of symbolic imagination corresponds to the synecdochic mode of figuration, where a part is taken as manifesting an essential attribute or quality of the whole and to the allegorical sense in medieval exegesis.

Ideologically, visionary Christianity in its attitude to history and social reality is akin to radicalism. It is radical in its belief in a total revolution or fundamental change, by which the present order will be reconstituted into an entirely new order, with a violent but cleansing elimination of the evils and injustices of the existing state of affairs. It is true that unlike political radicalism of a secular kind apocalyptic Christianity looks to an act of God to bring about the change. However, the confidence of much secular radicalism in the inevitable triumph of total justice implies a principle, such as the laws of history, transcending deliberate social and political action.

Secular and Christian radicalism are alike in the presence within them of an unresolved tension between the inevitability of the change and the imperative to work for its advent. That tension makes it difficult to say clearly what is the principal practical expression of the visionary version of Christian religion. The unshakable certitude of faith in the divine intervention and the coming of the final Kingdom would make passive expectation the appropriate response. And that has been the attitude in some visionary groups. But the revelation of God's plan to a privileged few would seem to call upon them to live already as if the old world were merely for destruction and the new world present by anticipation. Hence the violent revolutionary action of some apocalyptic sects. The contrast is similar to the conflict in Marxism between a deterministic view of history, which implies waiting for the process to pass through its stages, and the conviction that the revolution is to be led by a militant élite, who may therefore be able to modify the time and manner of its realization.[47]

Let me round off this account of visionary Christianity with a few historical remarks. The Christian religion, as I have said, began as a visionary message or *kerygma,* offering apocalyptic hope in a new order, against the background of social and political disorder and the confused fragmentation of the mythical worlds both of Judaism and of Hellenism. The intensity of expectation of the coming of Christ in glory to bring the final Kingdom died away as its fulfilment seemed indefinitely postponed. Meanwhile Christianity in its efforts to retain the distinctiveness of its beliefs and practices against the syncretism of its Gnostic rivals developed into a system of orthodoxy and as such took its place as part of the established order of the Roman Empire. With the breakup of that empire, the Church in the West emerged as the principal source of social and political authority. In that fashion, the predominant and official form of Christianity became the mythical, understanding itself as a total, all-embracing normative order, authoritatively representing the reality of the cosmos and nature, of human existence and history. Its interpretation was the prerogative of divinely appointed hierarchs. Nevertheless in every period of Christian history there were fringe groups or dissenting sects fostering some form of visionary or apocalyptic religion. In mainline Christianity itself the weakening of the power of Christian myth has been partly offset by a revival of interest in eschatology and in apocalyptic. Today there is a widespread tendency to regard the Christian religion as a radical, revolutionary force, subversive of every existing order and preaching the promise of the really new. Visionary Christianity has thus moved back from the fringe towards the center.

CHAPTER 6

Fourth Model: Mystical Christianity

In a sense this fourth version of the Christian religion takes us beyond Christianity, because everything distinctively Christian is relativized and treated as replaceable. What essentially constitutes the Christian religion in this mode of interpretation is an unmediated experience or apprehension of God—or, since the concept of God is itself dispensable, of the Godhead or Ultimate. At the same time we can speak of a Christian mysticism, because every experience is necessarily mediated and contextual. The unmediated experience of God or the Absolute is in reality a mediated immediacy, that is, a mediation in which the mediating elements become transparent, facilitating and not blocking a direct relationship with the experienced reality. The mediating elements cease to be an object of attention; they are left behind; they can be replaced by other mediatory elements, because they are not valued for their own sake.

Thus, insofar as the mystical experience takes place within a Christian context, it is seen as an immediate gift of God in which God freely leaves aside the normative Christian order and grants a direct communication with the divine self. Although in adapting itself to the requirements of Christian orthodoxy, the mystical mode of interpretation grants legitimacy to the Christian normative order and allows it a function in preparing people to enter upon the mystical ascent, in principle the Christian scheme of salvation is denied any real validity. Mystical contemplation is the sole means of union with God, and it is a means sufficient of itself. This equivalently denies the usefulness of all other religious activities, whether ritual or ascetical or good works in regard to the neighbour. Although the mystical union is a gift, it is granted to all who are ready to abandon all self-love and submit themselves passively to union with God.

The Christian scheme of salvation is left aside, not only by insistence upon passive contemplation as the only means of union with God, but also by the teaching on the necessity for a disinterested love of God that renounces all concern with personal salvation and on the loss of individuality at the height of mystical union. The love of God may begin as a sentiment or desire, but it becomes an identification with God in which the love of God is God's own love present and operative within the soul, so that all distinction is lost.

Good works in regard to our neighbor are made to take second place and should not be allowed to interfere with the pursuit of mystical contemplation. While the created world, both natural and social, is not necessarily regarded as evil, as in visionary Christianity (though such a conviction is occasionally found among the mystics), it, including human nature, is dismissed as incapable of either creating or participating in the values uniquely found in mystical contemplation and in the identification with God realized in it. There is thus a withdrawal from the processes of nature and of history and an exclusive concern with the mystical ascent.

The quietist devaluation of religious and moral activity proper to the mystical mode of interpretation in its pure form extends also to intellectual activity. Here a distinction must be made between mysticism itself and mystical theology. Mysticism itself or the mystical experience finds expression in lyrical, poetical, or unsystematized symbolic expression. Mystical theology or the attempted systematization of mystical knowledge is in fact the product of the attempt by orthodoxy to assimilate the mystical experience and integrate it into its own scheme. Even a writer like John of the Cross with a reputation as a trained theologian shows a complete lack of interest in theological speculation. He is content to give a general submission to the dogmas of the Catholic Church without any inclination to enter into the efforts of Scholastic theology to achieve a reflexive and systematic understanding and elaboration of those dogmas. He is concerned with a process of spiritual transformation, available in principle equally to the unlearned as well as to the learned. He remains within the framework of orthodoxy by his general acceptance of Church dogmas, but the dogmatic content of orthodoxy does not have any intrinsic relation to the process of mystical ascent. That is an affair of stages of passive contemplation, with the renunciation of the activity of all the faculties and eventually of the self itself.

I have suggested an affinity between the mystical version of the Christian religion and satire. The ground of the affinity is that both assume the inadequacy of all language, including the symbolic, and indeed see an ineluctable incongruity between consciousness and the conditions of life in this world. Insofar as mysticism retains the figure of Christ, he is spiritualized as the interior teacher, the light of the soul, or the interior lover, the unseen bridegroom. Satire as such is reserved for the normative claims of institutional Christianity, with its absurd appropriation of the Absolute, its spiritual pretensions, confusing means with the end, and its perennial hypocrisy. The root of the satirical attitude to official Christianity on the part of mysticism is its self-understanding as an independent religious principle. As Troeltsch puts it, mysticism "sees itself as the real universal heart of all religion, of which the various myth-forms are merely the outer garment."[48] Troeltsch also points out that mysticism "has an affinity with the autonomy of science, and it forms a refuge for the religious life of the cultured classes."[49] An historical continuity links modern rationalism with mysticism, rational autonomy with the autonomy of the inner light. Both are opposed in principle to orthodoxy, each demanding in its own way that one see for oneself.

The bearer, then, of knowledge and truth in the mystical version of Christianity is the autonomous individual, and the favored form of argumentation is contextualist, in which each line of thought is pursued into an ever-widening context of an abyss of meaning.

What becomes of the Church? In the last analysis there is no Church or community, because the mystical ascent takes place in the individual and then at the summit goes beyond individuality itself to identity. At a level below that of the final unity, the Church is the invisible, spiritual community of those illuminated by the light of mystical experience, a community that transcends all confessional differences. At a lower level still, the Church with its ascetical and ritual practices is allowed a preparatory and educative role, though this admission would seem to arise from the need somehow to integrate the mystical mode of interpretation into orthodoxy and is not fully coherent with the conviction that the sole means of union with God is passive contemplation, equally accessible to the simple and unlearned and to a learned religious élite.

There is in Bérulle a remarkable attempt to resolve the conflict between the direct communication with God proclaimed by the mystical mode of interpretation and the indirect, mediated role of communication proper to the ecclesiastical institution. He brings the Church under the concept of mission, which may be understood as an orthodox translation of the concept of emanation. The reality of Church as the continuation of the reality of the incarnate Son is the reality of a divine mission or emanation. The Father sent the Son as incarnate, and Father and Son sent the Spirit. The Church is the continuation of the Incarnation in the mission of the Spirit. The reality of the Church is that of a divine emanation, so that in the Church one can ascend through the missions into the unity of the Godhead.[50] In that fashion through the Platonic scheme of emanation, theologically translated into the doctrine of the divine missions, Bérulle was able to justify the permanent role of the humanity of Christ—a point that had long been troublesome to those attempting to integrate the mystical experience into orthodoxy—and the indispensable function of the hierarchical Church institution.

However, ideologically there is an affinity between mysticism in its usual forms and anarchism, inasmuch as neither recognizes any order outside the individual.

I will not conclude this account of the mystical version of the Christian religion with any historical remarks, because the history of mysticism within Christianity has often been recounted. I should like, however, to gather together the points made in the last four sections by extending the previous table with some additional entries.

Type of Christian religion	Mythical: total order as normative	Pragmatic: practical way of life	Visionary: new world in contrast to the old	Mystical: unmediated experience of the Absolute
Idea of the Church	Visible institution, part of divinely established order	Voluntary association in the public sphere	Visible group or sect as contingent, partial embodiment of invisible community of elect	Invisible spiritual communion
Bearer of knowledge and value	Visible Church as cultural community	The individual in the context of the critical public as a community of discourse	The elect or true believers	The autonomous individual
Christian action	Sacraments and ritual	Moral action in this world	Passive expectation / Revolutionary action	Withdrawal from action to passive contemplation

CHAPTER 7

Myth and Metaphysics

The reason for sketching the four preceding ideal types of Christian religion is to provide an instrument for reflection. The question behind the whole exposition is, What is the Christian religion? The realization that there was no single answer to that question, that Christianity has been a different thing at different times, in different places and to different people, led to the complex attempt I have just finished to order the data. But the question, What is the Christian religion? cannot be suitably asked or answered in a purely theoretical fashion. A more honest formulation would be, What is living and what is dead in Christianity for me today? The Christian religion is no longer a given, a taken-for-granted reality, which one simply accepts or rejects. History, the social sciences, studies of religious language: all these have brought to light the plurality of symbols, concepts, beliefs, and attitudes claiming the name of Christian. The disengagement of modern society, culture, and life from the Christian religion has left ordinary Christians the task of asking themselves which Christian elements they should try to rescue and bring into an effective relationship with their day-to-day existence. Whether one rejoices in the situation or deplores it, there is for the educated person no simple way of being a Christian in today's world.

What is living and what is dead in Christianity for me today? The question put in that way presupposes a static conception of the Christian religion. But Christianity is a dynamic reality, always changing. The governing question should be, What can Christianity become for us? The appraisal of the past and of the present is to uncover the resources that can lead us into the future. It is with that question in mind I offer a critical appraisal of each of the four models, discussing the limitations and possible contributions of each. The reflections are personal as they have to be. The question is not one that can be answered by a detached scholar—though scholarly knowledge has its relevance here—but only by those who are practically involved in the struggle to make Christianity effective in their lives. I am therefore writing for myself, but in union with the many Christians I know who are sharing the same struggle.

The question, then, as raised by the first model of Christian religion, the mythical, is, How far does and can the Christian religion provide a normative, comprehensive order, within which Christians can live out their lives? Or, to put it in another way, How far does the Christian symbolic system provide a basic encoding of human experience in today's world? For me, the Christian myth is no longer functioning in that all-embracing way.

Myth may be considered first as ethos and then as worldview. Ethos is the character and quality of the life of a people, the pervasive moral sentiments, the implicit beliefs embodied in ways of acting, in styles of thinking, in language and institutions. The elements that go into the production of an ethos as the prevailing spirit of a people are held together and transmitted by a set of basic images—images of the world, the family, the self, woman, child, warrior, king, and so on. These images coalesce into myth as worldview, which is the set of symbols (both images and stories) giving the most comprehensive picture of things as they actually are, the general conception of order that governs the life of a people. Ethos and worldview are mutually confirmatory. The prevailing moral sentiments are congruent with the worldview and thus are an experiential confirmation of it, and the worldview evokes those particular sentiments and confirms them as corresponding to the shape of reality.

Now, in my opinion, the ethos of our present society is unchristian. Christianity is no longer functioning as an ethos, even though elements, often distorted or enfeebled, continue to have some impact from our common Christian past. The situation of Christians today is that they are immersed in an unchristian ethos which, willy-nilly, pervades their day-to-day lives. They can live as Christians only by resisting the prevalent ethos and finding in their Christian convictions a transformative and critical principle. But this is equivalent to saying that they must interpret the Christian religion not as myth but according to one of the other models I have sketched.

But the difficulty is not simply that our individualist, possessive, competitive society is unchristian. It is that human social existence is dramatically at grips with a new set of problems, which threaten its very continuance but which cannot be overcome within the limits of traditional Christianity. Humanity has to break through to a new stage of existence beyond the assimilative capacity of the Christian myth, or it will perish. Take the following selection of issues: nuclear arms, the ecological crisis, the various liberation struggles, feminism, religious pluralism. Humanity has to come up with radically new and effectively operative images of power, nature, human solidarity, freedom, woman, revelation, and sacred authority. When I read Christian literature of the past or listen to sermons in the present, I am struck, as I am sure others are, by the lack of proportion between the problems we are facing and the traditional Christian images and attitudes. People, especially the liberation theologians, are reexamining the Christian heritage in an effort to exploit its hidden resources for meeting today's problems. Christianity can indeed change and develop. But the extent of the difficulty may perhaps be conveyed by the remark of Maurice Wiles that he knew of no version of the Incarnation that was "true to incarnational doctrine as understood in the past, while at the same time allowing a genuine openness to the positive significance of other faiths."[51]

That remark leads me to say why I find Karl Rahner's theology fundamentally unsatisfying, despite the brilliance that makes it the greatest theological achievement of our time. Although Rahner has tackled theologically almost every contemporary issue, his theology does not, I think, relate convincingly to the ethos of our present society. My reservation about it may be summed up in Rahner's own terminology. It is this: when it comes to the distinctively Christian claims, Rahner attempts to transfer to the categorical the certitude and universality that properly belong to the transcendental. To explain.

Rahner's entire theology rests upon a distinction between the transcendental and the categorial. "Transcendental" refers to the experience of subjects in the depths of subjectivity, prior to reflection and the experience of objects. It points to the dimension of human experience where there is an unthematic awareness of the wholeness of being. That awareness is implicitly present at the ordinary or categorial level of human knowing and willing. "Categorial" (or "categorical") refers to objective, historical experience of the particular and concrete. It constitutes the ordinary, everyday level of knowledge and decision making, with its specific or thematized content and changing history.

Now, according to the transcendental anthropology that lies at the center of Rahner's theology, every human person is the event of a supernatural self-communication of God. God's self-communication is human self-transcendence and vice versa. In other words, God is the horizon, copresent in an unobjectified fashion as the transcendental condition of possibility of the free acts by which the human person in self-transcendence moves towards fulfilment. That self-communication of God is supernatural and unmerited. It is grace. But in this concrete order it is given to every person, at least in the form of an offer. Hence the free subject possesses his or her freedom in the mode of "yes" or in the mode of "no" to God's self-communication. The "yes" is faith. Notice that both the self-communication of God and the fundamental option or response of faith take place on the level of transcendental experience, which can never be fully recaptured by reflection.

There is, then, a universal, transcendental revelation, coincident with the supernatural, unreflexive experience of God's self-communication. In contrast to it, there is special, categorial revelation, which consists in the historical objectification or thematization of that self-communication, the process, as it were, of its self-interpretation or its coming to articulate self-expression.

The distinction between the transcendental and the categorial levels of revelation and faith would seem at first sight to provide an excellent basis for finally overcoming Christian exclusiveness and acknowledging the legitimate and indeed necessary plurality of religious traditions and symbol systems at the historical, categorial level. While the unity and universality of the human relationship with the Ultimate or Beyond would be secured at the transcendental level, the categorial level would allow for the plurality and complementarity of traditions as found in the religious history of humankind. What is distinctively Christian, in contrast to, say, Buddhism or Judaism or other traditions, would seem to belong to the categorial level and thus without the universal claim proper to the transcendental. In that way, the universal incidence of supernatural faith and revelation would be reconciled with the particularity of the Christian revelation.

Rahner, however, does not draw that conclusion. He affirms a permanent and universal validity for the Christian articulation and objectification of transcendental revelation. He yields nothing of Christian exclusiveness and thus in effect gives the Christian revelation on the categorial level the unchanging permanence, universal validity and unshakable certitude that belong properly to the transcendental level.

That is well illustrated by his famous thesis on "anonymous Christians." In its basic affirmation, the thesis is not particularly original. Catholic theologians have long acknowledged that the universal saving will of God is operative as offering salvation to every human person. Rahner does indeed stress—though other theologians have done the same—that the offer of salvation and the response to that offer cannot take place in the individual non-Christian in a completely ahistorical and asocial way. To suppose so would be to undermine the basis for affirming the historical and social nature of Christianity itself. Consequently, as Rahner argues, non-Christian religions as the social and historical expression of the moral and religious life of non-Christians must be understood as having a role to play in mediating supernatural faith, hope, and love to non-Christians. With this point, Rahner does go beyond what has been traditionally taught under the heading of the baptism of desire. Non-Christians who lived according to their conscience were thought of as being saved despite the religions to which they belonged, rather than because of them. Rahner, therefore, with other recent theologians sees no reason to deny a positive saving function to non-Christian religions. So far so good. But Rahner shows the distance he stands from any frank acknowledgment of the pluralism in unity of religious history by hastening to add:

> Nor is there any question of making such a religion equal to Christian faith in its salvific significance, nor of denying its depravity or its provisional character

in the history of salvation, nor of denying that such a concrete religion can also have negative effects on the event of salvation in a particular non-Christian.[52]

In other words, faith has everywhere a Christological character. It comes in and through Jesus Christ. That is the justification for speaking of an anonymous Christianity. Where there is faith, there is Christianity, even though it is not recognized as such and even when it has not been fully realized according to its proper nature. Other traditions have but a provisional and subordinate function, nor do they have the purity of essence of the Christian revelation.

The equivalently transcendental claim thus made for the Christian revelation in its particularity and distinction from other religious traditions has questionable effects throughout the whole of Rahner's theology. As noticed by the advocates of political theology in their reaction against Rahner's program for a transcendental theology, this claim removes Christian realities from the concrete context of society and history. This is especially evident in its treatment of the Church, where the distinction between the transcendental and the categorial becomes a distinction between a permanent essence of the Church and its phenomenal existence, between an unchanging self-identity and its varying performance in the concrete, so that only on the phenomenal level is there an historical dialectic and the essence of the Church is removed from history. The result is a fundamentally uncritical theology, because the transcendental claims made for Christian revelation precisely as Christian cannot be rooted in a universal transcendental experience and become, instead, arbitrary assertions.

Hence Rahner's theology, despite his valiant attempts to come to grips with the detailed issues confronting men and women today, remains remote from the contemporary, pluralistic mentality.

Before this digression on Rahner, I was arguing that our present society was confronting problems that could not be met within the limits of traditional Christianity. Whatever the potential of a transformed Christianity in the future, it is not at present functioning as the ethos of our society, namely, as determining the character and quality of its life through pervasive moral sentiments and the implicit beliefs embodied in ways of acting. Nor in its present form is it capable of doing so. Rahner's theology shows how answers to contemporary issues from the narrow context of traditional Christianity fail to convince in today's pluralistic context. Insofar as Christianity is still the pervasive ethos in, say, some conservative Roman Catholic environments or in Protestant fundamentalist groups, it is woefully out of keeping with the realities of human existence today. We must look to Christianity as a transformative principle for the future, not as an existing ethos.

The second function of myth is to serve as worldview, namely, as a comprehensive picture or encoding of things as they actually are. The question of the viability of the Christian myth is related to the transition from myth to metaphysics, from metaphysics to theory of knowledge and from theory of knowledge to deconstruction.

The transition from myth to metaphysics occurs with what Voegelin calls the Hellenic rupture, in which the compact or undifferentiated mythical order was broken open by the emergence of autonomous reason. This rupture corresponds to the shift to theory in Lonergan's account of the stages of meaning.[53] (Two other ruptures in the original, compact mythical universe may be distinguished: the monotheistic rupture in Israel, making God as transcendent distinct from the universe, and the mystical rupture in India, differentiating the term of mystical experience from the world of change.[54] But, although these two ruptures introduce a discontinuity within the comprehensive mythical order, they do not cancel the functioning of myth as the metaphorical encoding or representation of the total order of reality as experienced, whereas the break through to reason and theory displaces myth,)

When independent reason or reason as the source of its own, rational criteria took over the task of constructing a comprehensive account of reality, metaphysics was created as a general theory of being or ontology. Whereas the procedure of myth was the synthesizing of images by similarity and dissimilarity, the thrust of theory was to drive through to the literal meaning underlying the representation and to formulate that meaning in precise concepts, which were then ordered systematically. The basic concepts formed into a system constituted metaphysics. The other sciences or branches of theoretical knowledge, namely, physics, biology, and psychology, were conceived as bringing successive determinations to the concepts and statements of metaphysics. They were not therefore autonomous sciences but part of philosophy and subordinate to metaphysics.[55]

When Christianity entered into a public relation with Hellenistic culture, becoming in a remarkably short time its exclusive religion, the problem was how to relate the Christian myth as worldview to the theoretical worldview of metaphysical philosophy. At first this was a question for the few. The elaboration of the Christian gospel into the Christian myth as a comprehensive picture of reality served as the general framework of thought and life at least as far as the Renaissance, if not beyond. The coherence of the Christian myth was not seriously affected by the assimilation of elements, such as the immortality of the soul, from the preceding Hellenistic world view. But the tension between Christianity functioning as myth and reason as it had emerged in the Hellenistic rupture came down to the Middle Ages as the problem of reason and revelation or reason and faith. The problem led to the development of ontotheology, conspicuously most successful in Thomas Aquinas. Ontotheology is the attempt to translate the content of the Christian myth into the theoretical concepts and statements of metaphysical philosophy.

From the religious point of view, there are three difficulties with ontotheology. First is its intellectualism. It makes knowledge not love foundational. This is the religious counterpart to the objection that it makes theory not practice foundational. I will come back to this point in dealing with the shift from metaphysics to theory of knowledge.

Second, it presupposes the possibility of abstracting the literal meaning from religious symbols and formulating it in the precise, technical concepts of systematic reason. Thus it is deemed possible, if only by analogy and extrapolation, to elaborate concepts of God as Pure Act, of the incarnate *esse* of Jesus Christ, of grace as supernatural habit, and so on, and then to build these concepts into a systematic theology. I think there is some reason to deny this possibility. The possession of meaning by religious symbols does not entail that their meaning can be translated into the concepts of metaphysical discourse. Their meaning refers to transcendent realities beyond human understanding; it is glimpsed through the experience evoked by the images. It cannot be disengaged from that experience and transcribed into a conceptuality articulated by theoretical intelligence. In that way it is closer to the meaning found in a work of art than that of a scientific treatise. No doubt the symbols give rise to thought. They call for interpretation, commentary, and criticism; they need to be related to other areas of meaning. But none of this allows for a conceptualization that would replace the symbols as an adequate transcription of their meaning. The theology of original sin did not succeed in conceptualizing the myth of Adam's fall.

The third religious difficulty with ontotheology is that it involved the Christian myth in the eventual downfall of metaphysics. As time went on, ontotheology had gradually replaced the Christian myth in the ordinary life of Christians. It thus killed the myth. If one looks at the catechisms, books of instruction, and sermons from before the recent biblical and liturgical revivals, one will see that what they give is a watered-down metaphysical theology, not the potent images and stories of a myth. The technical concepts of ontotheology had slowly worked their way down into popular religion. They blocked the functioning of the myth, offering instead a pseudocertitude and precision. The demise of metaphysics thus became a religious crisis. Once a myth has been strangled by excessive speculation, there is no ready means of reviving it.

The reign of metaphysics came to an end when the sciences as autonomous separated themselves from philosophy. As autonomous, they established their own basic concepts for themselves, and did not turn to philosophy or recognize the hegemony of metaphysics. Since the sciences claimed between them to cover every area of reality, and since metaphysical entities were denied as not subject to scientific, that is, empirical, investigation, the concepts of metaphysics were emptied of reference. Kant responded to that situation by making philosophy foundational in the guise of theory of knowledge. Critical philosophy by laying down the conditions of possibility and limits of all our knowledge provided a foundation upon which the sciences could build and upon which they could rest in claiming objectivity and truth. The historical development here was complex,[56] but what eventually emerged after Hegel with the neo-Kantians was the notion of philosophy as *Erkenntnis-theorie* or theory of knowledge, sitting in judgment upon the empirical sciences as grounding their methods; distinguishing, relating, and unifying their respective spheres of meaning; and determining the validity of their truth-claims as objective knowledge.

Bernard Lonergan in *Insight*[57] has produced a brilliant variation upon this notion of philosophy as a foundational account of knowledge. He avoids the difficulty of the self-grounding of epistemology, which has dogged it since Hegel's critique of Kant, by distinguishing cognitional theory from epistemology. Cognitional theory answers the question, What am I doing when I am knowing? and is verified as fact in the data of consciousness; epistemology asks, Why is doing that knowing? and looks back to cognitional theory for grounding. What, therefore, is now claimed as foundational is the invariant cognitional structure in human consciousness, a structure made explicit in cognitional theory. Cognitional theory, once articulated, is beyond any but merely incidental revision, because revision would have to follow the same cognitional structure it was attempting to revise. Philosophy, therefore, remains foundational by becoming unrevisable cognitional theory, though Lonergan sees its primary task as the practical one of guiding the self-appropriation of the invariant structure of our cognitional consciousness. Further, the concepts of metaphysics, emptied of their content by the sciences, are now given a function as empty. They are taken as heuristic notions, anticipating the structure of the known through a claimed isomorphism of knowing and the known. Metaphysics is thus retained and defended as the complete set of general heuristic notions. These correspond to cognitional acts as their objective counterparts, outlining the structure of what will be known when they are performed. Thus, in an heuristic and anticipatory way, metaphysics answers the question, what do I know when I perform my cognitional acts? The empty heuristic structures of metaphysics, which give us the structures of the known in anticipatory outline, are filled with actual knowledge of contingent reality by the different sciences. Admittedly, despite the originality of his approach, the metaphysics set forth by Lonergan remains remarkably traditional. Nevertheless it is newly grounded, namely, upon cognitional theory or, to be more precise, upon the invariant structure of cognitional consciousness as articulated in an allegedly unrevisable cognitional theory.

I had already left the Gregorian University, Rome, when Lonergan came there. I did not therefore come under his personal influence as a teacher. I came to his thought through reading. Elsewhere[58] I have described the very great influence Lonergan's thought had upon me in transforming the confused jumble of Scholastic theology and philosophy I had received into a dynamic inheritance, from which I could start and through which I could move in my own intellectual development. Despite, however, a constant temptation over some years to accept his basic contentions and become, like many contemporaries with a similar background to mine, a Lonerganian, something within me always held me back. What prevented me, I think, from following him as a disciple was the implausibility of finding a substantially unchanged Catholic dogmatic tradition at the end of the elaborate intellectual itinerary he sketched. As with Hegel's absolute knowledge, I suspected that Catholic dogma was found at the end of the journey because it had been there at the beginning and had accompanied Lonergan all along the way. In other words, behind Lonergan's search for an invariant basis of human knowing and his insistence that he had discovered an unrevisable cognitional theory and metaphysics lay his prior acceptance of the Catholic dogmatic tradition. He has not questioned that tradition in any fundamental fashion but sought instead to secure it.[59] I had my own reasons for disputing the claims of that tradition; and so, despite his powerful influence upon me, Lonergan did not meet my objections to the Roman Catholic Church, because he simply assumed what I questioned. The conclusion I drew was that his overriding concern to keep Catholic dogmas as unchanging truths in an age of relativism and historicism had been a chief factor leading Lonergan to discover—a bit too easily—an invariant basis for knowledge and an unrevisable cognitional theory and metaphysics.

For me the flaw in Lonergan's argument for the unrevisability of his cognitional theory lies in the supposition that to work out a scheme of cognitional activities on the basis of the data of consciousness is to have discovered and formulated all the elements of determining importance in human knowledge in the concrete. Let us grant that the structures of human cognitional consciousness are invariant. Between these invariant structures as data and cognitional theory as knowledge come their discovery, distinguishing, formulation, and verification. Since all this may be carried out more or less accurately, cognitional theory remains open to debate and revision. A revision may be "incidental" in relation to the basic scheme, which it leaves untouched, but of the weightiest consequence in relation to actual human knowing. Suppose, for example, one omits the section on belief from *Insight.* Since belief as communicated knowledge is more extensive than immanently generated knowledge even in the scientific knowledge possessed by the scientist, the omission of a consideration of belief would have made the account of knowledge in *Insight* so unbalanced as to lead inevitably to false conclusions about the concrete knowing process. Yet its omission would not have altered the basic scheme of Lonergan's cognitional theory. Again, the shift from *Insight* to *Method in Theology*, in which the fourth level of intentional consciousness, the level of decision and action, becomes the focus and conversion becomes foundational, is in my estimation a major change in the understanding and conceptualization of the process of human knowing, but it leaves intact Lonergan's basic scheme.

In brief, I do not think that Lonergan has succeeded in placing cognitional theory and, consequently, metaphysics beyond the inaccuracies and uncertainties, the pressures of self-interest and group bias, which mark all human knowledge. One can indeed question whether Lonergan's own cognitional theory is a sound, adequate, and balanced thematization of human knowing in all its concrete richness and complexity. But even if it were to emerge as the best available account, that would not make it unrevisable. Despite the valuable contribution that Lonergan has undoubtedly made to the clarification of many issues, he has not, in my opinion, provided a secure basis for the restoration of traditional metaphysics and Catholic ontotheology.

The reason for dwelling upon Lonergan's thought at this juncture is that *Insight* contains a worldview in the sense of a unified and comprehensive understanding of world process, and that worldview, as we shall see, has some right to be considered a Christian conception. The worldview is not a claim to a knowledge of everything in the world. For Lonergan, human knowledge is itself an ongoing process. His worldview is therefore presented as a generic account, which expresses the overall order or design and thus the intelligibility of world process, not the knowledge of the actual events in their concrete unfolding. It is based on the assumptions and methods of the sciences, rather than on their content.

The generic design or intelligibility of world process is given as emergent probability.[60] This brings together the fact of system and the fact of the nonsystematic or random into one explanatory idea. Lonergan's own account is concise, so that it is not easy to summarize further without losing all clarity for the uninitiated reader. To gain some understanding, one must grasp the meaning of schemes of recurrence, conditioned series of schemes of recurrence, and the probability of emergence and survival of schemes of recurrence.

Schemes of recurrence: There are regularly occurring events in the universe. The regularity comes from the combination of laws, ordering events into schemes of recurrence. A scheme of recurrence is a series of events in an order of succession such that each event in the series fulfills the conditions for the occurrence of the next event, and the occurrence of the last event fulfils the conditions for the recurrence of the first. There is thus a circular relationship between events, so that, other things being equal, they recur indefinitely. The examples Lonergan gives[61] of schemes of recurrence are the planetary system, the circulation of water over the earth, the nitrogen cycle, the routines of animal life.

Schemes of recurrence themselves fall into a conditioned series such that the earlier can function without the later, but the later cannot emerge or function unless the earlier are already functioning. The schemes constituting animal life could not have emerged unless earlier physico-chemical schemes were already functioning.

A scheme of recurrence acquires a probability of emergence as an earlier scheme provides the conditions for it to emerge, and it becomes more and more probable as more and more conditions for its emergence as a higher scheme are actually fulfilled. Likewise, an already functioning scheme of recurrence acquires a probability of survival. Although the scheme itself is regular through the circular relationships of the events in it, the repetition of the circle depends upon the continuance of the conditions that led to its emergence.

That brings us to Lonergan's brief definition: "Emergent probability is the successive realization in accord with successive schedules of probability of a conditioned series of schemes of recurrence."[62] This gives system its place in world process, inasmuch as the schemes of recurrence are the functioning of a combination of systematic or classical laws, and the nonsystematic its place, inasmuch as the emergence and survival of the schemes take place not systematically but in accord with probabilities.

Consequently world process is open, as a succession of probable realizations of possibilities. The conception is not deterministic, though there is order or design. Again, it is a developmental conception, allowing for the emergence of the new, but it admits breakdowns and blind alleys as well as progress.

Emergent probability as an explanation of world process is first and paradigmatically presented in the context of the natural sciences, in dealing with the complementarity of classical investigations, which regard the systematic, and statistical investigations, which regard the nonsystematic. Its application, however, is not limited to physical processes. The same basic idea of process underlies Lonergan's account (1) of knowledge as a dynamic structure of recurrent and related operations, open to the emergence of fresh results; (2) of the successive levels of development and functioning in the individual person, including practical and moral activity and the orientation to the transcendent; (3) of the ongoing process of history, with its possibilities and probabilities for progress and decline; (4) of the supernatural solution to the problem of evil and the human incapacity for sustained development. One could continue; it is possible to discern the basic idea of process, set forth as emergent probability, underlying every area of Lonergan's thought. It is truly a worldview.

Lonergan's worldview is metaphysical, because of the kind of thinking it represents, granted the qualification that for Lonergan metaphysics presupposes cognitional theory. But his worldview claims in two key respects to be also a Christian worldview.

It can be named Christian, first, because the account of knowledge on which it rests, usually called critical realism, may also be designated as Christian realism, according to the contention of Lonergan in his essay "The Origins of Christian Realism,"[63] that it is a necessary implication of the truth-claim of Christian dogma. In other words, in defending the truth of the doctrines of the Trinity and the Incarnation, Christians were led implicitly to presuppose "that the reality of the world mediated by meaning was known not by experience alone, not by ideas alone or in conjunction with experience, but by true judgements and beliefs."[64] That is the implicit presupposition which is articulated explicitly in Lonergan's cognitional theory and is the foundation for the idea of emergent probability.

The second reason for calling Lonergan's worldview Christian is that in the redemptive process of grace, which he sees as a harmonious continuation of the actual order of the universe,[65] he discerns the same generic intelligibility he analyzes as emergent probability in the context of the natural sciences. What we are therefore presented with is a metaphysico-theological synthesis that brings together contemporary science, both the natural and the social sciences, history, ethics, and Christian theology as all concerned with various levels of the same world process, which manifests throughout the same generic intelligibility.

No summary can convey the power of Lonergan's thought as it drives relentlessly onward from the assumptions and methods of contemporary science through the practical, moral, and religious workings of human intelligence to the underlying intelligibility of the Christian account of salvation and the supposedly invulnerable cognitional theory. But enough has been said to raise in a serious fashion two general questions: What is the status of such a worldview in relation to Christian faith? How far does the elaboration of a Christian worldview meet the needs of Christians in today's culture?

I may note in passing that the same questions could be raised concerning Teihard de Chardin's synthesis of modern science and Christian belief. But his work is intellectually much less powerful and fertile than Lonergan's. I think that Teilhard's synthesis is best characterized as a restatement of the Christian myth, using modern science symbolically. It is an attempted remythicization of Christian belief, whereas Lonergan tries to transcribe the Christian myth into a metaphysical conceptuality. Teilhard's work fails to convince because the Christian myth is no longer functioning effectively in modern society and a myth cannot be restored to life by an individual genius but only by a social transformation. Hence I have found when presenting the work of Teilhard to a group of students with diverse backgrounds that they find

Teilhard's writings implausible and fanciful. Lonergan presents a much more serious intellectual challenge. What he in effect argues, and argues well, is that if one examines the methods and assumptions of contemporary science, one will reach an understanding of human intelligence such that it will enable one to make sense of all further developments of human thought, including Christian dogma, even though the truth of dogma is a matter of supernatural belief, not of rational demonstration. Among the further developments is the idea of world process, the generic intelligibility of which may be extended to include the process of redemption.

What, then, is the relation of Lonergan's metaphysico-theological synthesis to Christian faith? Like any such synthesis, it is a transitory construction, which does not and cannot possess the absoluteness that belongs to faith itself. The absoluteness of faith is the absoluteness of total demand and total response in an experience of unrestricted love in relation to hidden transcendence or mystery. Faith is the drive toward transcendence, the thrust of human beings out of and beyond themselves, out of and beyond all the limited orders and human certainties under which they live, in an attempt to open themselves to the totality of existence and reach unlimited reality and ultimate value. It is a total response to the felt reality of a total demand. That absoluteness of faith should not be confused with a certitude of beliefs.

Faith, while possessing the assurance of a lived relationship, does not intellectually give absolute certitude. The certitude of propositional beliefs remains a limited, human certitude. The believer in being certain of a doctrine may have grounds for excluding error in that particular instance. Error, however, remains in principle a possibility. In religious matters as in others, as human beings we have to live with the constant recurrence of error. Lonergan here, unlike myself, accepts the Catholic claim that its dogmas are preserved free from error by the infallibility of the *magisterium*. There is further the difficult necessity of taking account of continuous changes in the cultural context that alter the meaning of terms and the way in which doctrines are understood. This may call for a thoroughgoing reconstruction of doctrinal formulations if they are to retain any valid meaning. Lonergan does not deny the impact of cultural changes but tries to introduce a large measure of unrevisability through his cognitional theory and his insistence that a particular judgment is an unconditional affirmation of truth through the fulfillment of the conditions for its truth in the particular, limited case, even though numerous other questions remain unanswered. Hence a judgment or propositional belief keeps its permanent validity in different cultural contexts.

The argument, one feels, could go on indefinitely. The real issue here involves two fundamentally different ways of intellectually living the Christian faith.

Those who like myself follow the first way are filled with an ineluctable awareness of the ambiguities and contradictions of human experience. They do not see Christian faith as removing the ambiguities or resolving the contradictions but as providing a basic assurance through which we can live with love and trust in the midst of the inescapable negativities and unanswered questions of human existence. All our knowledge is tainted by sin, self-interest, and group bias and marred by the imperfection and failure of every human endeavour. Religious knowledge is no exception. The more elaborate our theological constructions, the further removed they are from that basic experience, and hence the less reliance we should place in them. The very sweep and relentless logic of Lonergan's synthesis creates in those who follow the first way a sense of distrust and a drawing back before what they fear as intellectual hubris.

Those, however, who follow the second way focus upon Christian faith as purifying, strengthening, and raising on to a new level the power of the human intellect. Christian revelation and grace are taken as providing the essential solution to the human predicament, a solution rendered permanent in human history through the Church. The believer through an acceptance of authoritatively transmitted and interpreted propositional beliefs is provided with a basic set of religious certainties. Through grace human intelligence is offered release from the biases that afflict it. Possessed of the essential truths concerning the human condition and intellectually converted by grace, the believer can proceed to despoil the Egyptians in the sense of incorporating the latest findings of the secular sciences, duly purified and corrected, into a vast metaphysico-theological synthesis or worldview.

An intellectual style is not chosen arbitrarily. I should like, therefore, at the cost of some repetition, to try to make clear why syntheses such as Lonergan's do not work for me and for others. They do not meet the needs I have as a Christian in the unchristian culture of today.

Any metaphysico-theological synthesis depends upon the Christian myth and its functioning. The dependence is not reciprocal. Even in the heyday of Christendom, no one theology or philosophy succeeded in gaining universal adherence. The vigorous attempts of the papacy in the nineteenth and twentieth centuries to impose Thomism by disciplinary measures failed. In the actual life of the Christian Church, metaphysical theologies—there are always a number—have a secondary role and a relative, transitory validity. The more intellectually ambitious the theology, the less plausibility it can draw from the myth at its basis. Already the doctrinalization of the Christian myth, namely the translation of the myth into propositional beliefs, imposed as dogmas, created a top-heavy structure, which the myth was not designed to carry. In regard both to doctrines and their metaphysico-systematic elaborations, one is provoked to say that they are attempts to express what cannot be expressed in the fashion chosen. At the present time, the Christian myth is functioning only fitfully if at all, owing to cultural changes, which have both weakened its plausibility and stifled the religious imagination. The appropriate response would seem to be a renewal of Christian practice in the context of ordinary life, social, political, and cultural, and a consequent rebirth of images to express on the basis of Christian practice a Christian perception of our present situation.

Knowledge is not foundational. It does not, as *Erkenntnistheorie* or theory-of-knowledge approach would have it, provide a fixed basis for the rest of conscious human living. Knowledge is not a privileged element, which stands apart as an independent origin or source, a point of reference for the entirety of human existence. Knowledge is a social and historical product, inseparably interwoven with the whole round of activities and relations that constitute the structure and history of the society of the knowers. To put it in another way, knowledge is not a reality apart from praxis; it is not a realm or world of its own, proceeding purely by its own laws as an independent totality; it is an element within praxis itself, so that modes of knowledge, scientific or metaphysical, are to be understood in the context of the other elements and relationships that constitute praxis as a totality. By praxis here I mean the embodied activities of socially related men and women, whereby they struggle with nature as a reality independent of consciousness and with the sedimented, objectified products of past human action, in order to shape their world and themselves in their world.

The refusal to make knowledge a privileged, independent element means that a deep disorder—as at present—in the functioning of knowledge or consciousness can be cured not theoretically or by a critique of consciousness but only by a change in the social order and in people's mode of life. It is not that one is advocating mindless activism; theoretical activity is itself an important part of praxis but that one gives up the illusion of stepping outside the structure of language, signs, history, social relationships, onto a fixed base in consciousness, from which the changes in the other elements can be absolutely evaluated.

How far does the development in Lonergan's own thought meet the objections I have raised to his metaphysico-theological synthesis? Let me first admit that there has been an immense shift in his thought—so immense that I personally do not think that he fully measured all its implications. My account of his world view was based on *Insight*. In *Method in Theology* and subsequent articles the intellectualism of *Insight* is considerably modified. As I have already remarked, what becomes foundational is conversion, and although intellectual conversion is identified with intellectual self-appropriation as urged by *Insight*, a prior dependence in the concrete of intellectual conversion upon moral and religious conversion is admitted. Further, besides the knowledge derived empirically from below upwards, namely, from experience through understanding to judgment, there is faith as the knowledge born of love, which moves from above downwards, namely, from love down through cognitional operations to achieve a discernment and healing of bias and inauthenticity. In other words, besides the generalized empirical method, put forward in *Insight* and providing the underlying structure of *Method in Theology,* Lonergan introduces the concept of praxis as a method called for now that the age of innocence is over and authenticity can no longer be taken for granted.[66] Praxis, according to Lonergan, is the sublation of the cognitional process by deliberation, evaluation, decision, and action, and it effects a discernment between the products, including cognitional products, of human authenticity and the products of human inauthenticity.

What has happened, it seems to me, is that, whereas in *Insight* according to any straightforward interpretation knowledge was foundational, love is now seen as foundational, and in the present concrete order of sin and redemption that love is a transcendent gift of the Spirit. Without that love, human knowledge is mired in inauthenticity. I cannot but agree with the shift from knowledge to love as foundational. It corresponds to my own conviction, which reading Lonergan has helped me to articulate. But I remain dissatisfied with Lonergan's presentation, because of what I sense is a deep inconsistency in his approach.

First, Lonergan does not do justice to the social and political dimensions of praxis. What he offers us is essentially a philosophy of consciousness, in which the inner events or states of consciousness are always the independent variables, of which everything else in human living and history is a function. What he says about the Church and the future of Christianity is representative, I think, of his general attitude to human affairs: "the perpetually needed remedy is not outer but inner."[67] That expresses a dichotomy the recent concept of praxis was designed to exclude.

Second, Lonergan remains an incurable dogmatist, in the sense of seeking and claiming unrevisable certainties. Almost as soon as he introduces the concept of faith as a knowledge born of love he hastens to rejoin the Christian dogmatic tradition. Among the values faith discerns, he argues, is the value of believing. Hence by faith one enters into the religious community as a community of belief, which is a higher collaboration of men and women in disseminating the judgments of fact and the judgments of value proposed for their acceptance by the word of religion.[68] His earlier detour through cognitional theory led back to the traditional Scholastic metaphysics. His more recent detour through faith-love brings him back to the familiar Catholic dogmas. In the end was my beginning.

I have dwelt with what some will regard as disproportionate length upon the metaphysico-theological synthesis of Lonergan because his work for me and for many others in North America represents the one form in which ontotheology remains a feasible option. The previous discussion of it, therefore, allows me now to generalize about philosophico-religious worldviews without a vagueness due to lack of any concrete reference.

A worldview, bringing to bear all the resources of reason upon the data of faith to form a comprehensive synthetic account of reality, the world, and the human situation, is at best a possible cultural consequence of Christian faith, possessing some probability and some measure of intellectual usefulness. It should never however be identified with the Christian faith. The mythical form of the Christian religion is itself, though of venerable antiquity, a transitory cultural product. Neither it nor its articulation into a set of doctrines is identical with the Christian faith. The Christian religion may create, and has indeed created, worldviews, but it is in the core of its identity neither a mythical nor a metaphysical worldview. Its essential religious content is not an intellectual answer to the questions raised by the human condition; it does not clear up the ambiguities and contradictions that surround human existence. What it gives is the reality of transcendent love, made manifest in Jesus Christ, and mediated by set of images and stories. These guide practice, but fall short of a comprehensive picture of reality. Christian faith is a transforming principle, not a body of objective knowledge.

The present situation, as I read it, is that, owing to the fragmentation of knowledge and the erosion of the Western cultural heritage through the pervasive dominance of a merely instrumental rationality, the elaboration in a grounded intellectual fashion of a comprehensive worldview is generally considered an overambitious enterprise, even when it is not dismissed as impossible in principle. Serious thinkers remain within their specialty and leave the popularizers to produce their semiimaginative syntheses of science, philosophy, and religion, with occasionally a dash of the occult. As far as religion itself is concerned, the Christian myth, together with its transcription into doctrines, is not functioning well; it has largely lost its accent of reality. This is partly because it has broken down as a synthesis through the failure of the Christian Churches and their members to assimilate new knowledge and new experiences and partly because of the obsolescence of some of the fundamental Christian images. To illustrate the latter problem, take so simple an example of Christian God-language as the *Our Father*; it presupposes a set of social relationships no longer ours today. "Our Father who art in heaven"—without patriarchy, fatherhood does not evoke transcendence; "Hallowed be thy name"—the names of rulers are not exalted, save in some survivals of archaic ceremonial; "Thy kingdom come"—kingly rule is no longer a reality; "Thy will be done on earth as it is in heaven"—society is not an affair of a single will, but of consensus; "Give us this day our daily bread"—we consider we have a right to the necessities of life without asking for them as bounty; "And forgive us our debts as we also have forgiven our debtors"—our debts in present society are not to persons, from whom we can beg remission, but from banks, which simply blacklist our credit cards; "And lead us not into temptation", which means "Do not put us to the test"—we no longer have to prove ourselves worthy servants before a lord and master; "But deliver us from evil, that is, the Evil One"—we have learned not to project our shadow side, but to integrate it.

In brief, religiously we need a process of desymbolization and of resymbolization, arising out of a renewal of Christian experience in the context of modern society, rather than the production of any metaphysico-theological syntheses, which are rendered implausible by the present state of the Christian religion. Whatever its defects, liberation theology has perceived the necessity of living out the Christian faith in relation to the social and political reality of our daily lives and finding thereby a renewal of theology. When we turn away from the blandishments of metaphysics or cognitional theory and from the search for a fixed base on which to build impregnable intellectual castles for ourselves, we meet today the deconstructionists, who, outdoing Heidegger, have mounted the most powerful attack yet on the whole Western philosophical tradition from Plato onwards.[69]

The word "deconstruction" was first used by Jacques Derrida to identify his own way of dealing with a text. Ignoring forerunners, we may see the contemporary movement of deconstruction as beginning with Derrida's *De la grammatologie,* published in 1967. From philosophy and literary criticism, the movement has now penetrated into theology[70] and biblical studies.[71]

For a rough placing, we may note that deconstruction is post-structuralist in its resolute refusal of the idea of structure as somehow objectively in a text and reflecting an invariant pattern in the human mind. With hermeneutic philosophy *à la* Heidegger the relationship is more complex. On the one hand, Heidegger's *Destruktion* would seem to pursue a similar end to Derrida's *deconstruction.* On the other hand, Derrida does not think Heidegger's interpretive method radical enough. Heidegger, he argues, reappropriates the metaphysical tradition he intends to overcome. The key question between them is, "Which comes first, Being or language?" Heidegger places the source of thought in the moment of Being, the plentitude or presence, which precedes or effaces articulate discourse. For Derrida a quest for truth, origins, presence outside the endless play of language is a delusion. He does not seek a ground of meaning and truth in Being, but aims at releasing a multiplicity of meanings through the limitless free play of significations.

What, then, is the antimetaphysical complaint of the deconstructionists? It is that philosophers have ignored or suppressed the disruptive and distancing effect of language and only thereby been able to impose their systems. Western metaphysics is built upon the illusion that reason can leave behind language and reach the pure presence of truth and reality. Derrida speaks of it as a metaphysics of presence. What is truly real for the metaphysicians is what presents itself immediately and fully to the knowing mind. But can one thus escape language and the disruptive effect of language?

Saussure distinguished in the linguistic sign two components, the signifier or material component (namely, the phonetic element) and the signified or mental component (namely, the image or concept). Now the relation between signifier and signified is arbitrary, and the signifiers are thus independent of the meanings we attach to them. Hence there is no guarantee that we can always say what we mean or mean what we say. There is a rupture betwen the signifiers we use and the meanings we intend. There is no immediate and full presence of the signified to the signifier. Further, because signifiers are independent, writers are not in complete control of their own language.

But if there is a distance which cannot be overcome because of the very nature of language between signifiers and the signified, then the relation of reference between the sign as a whole and the reality it claims to represent is also disrupted. Consequently there is no extralinguistic reality to which the verbal signs unambiguously refer or which they make present. Both meaning and being are endlessly distanced or deferred by the language in which we claim to represent them.

Languages are in fact systems of internal differences, not sets of references to a reality that has its own meaning outside the relations of the linguistic systems. In Derrida's phrase, there is no "transcendental signified"—there is no absolute reality, made present in language, that has and imposes its own independent meaning, not produced by the linguistic system of differences.

Derrida is here taking over and elaborating Saussure's point about the arbitrary nature of both components of the linguistic sign. There is no intrinsic property that determines either the signifier or the signified or the relation between them. For any signifier to express meaning, it must differ from the other signifiers in the language, and it is that difference alone that fixes its identity. Likewise each signified in a language must differ from all others, and it is that difference alone that determines its meaning. Language is a system of differences of sound combined with a system of differences of ideas. Outside the play of differential significations, linked to the system of differentially identified signifiers, there is no meaning. Or, to put it in another way, meaning is constantly deferred by the endless play of differences.

Armed with that understanding of language, Derrida develops a critique of the Western philosophical tradition as logocentric. In rejecting logocentrism, Derrida is repudiating both the classical *logos* as the voice of reason and the Christian *logos* as the voice of God. Saussure he sees as marking the end of the long logocentric epoch, though Saussure himself, Derrida argues, did not manage to shake off its hold. As dominant, logocentrism determined the history of metaphysics and the forms of science. Because it assigned the origin of truth to the *logos* or spoken word, rational or revelatory, it identified being as presence and regarded the object of science and metaphysics as present entities.

Another formulation of the same critique, a formulation which has been singled out as especially characteristic of Derrida, dubs the Western tradition as phonocentric, inasmuch as it gives a privileged place to speech, elevating the voice over writing, which is downgraded as secondary or derivative. Logocentrism and phonocentrism imply each other, because speech is regarded as superior and writing treated as debased speech under the illusion that speech communicates presence, whereas writing marks an absence. In Derrida's view of language, writing is not secondary but primordial; it precedes language and comprehends language. Derrida is not just inverting the phonocentric hierarchy and making writing in the ordinary sense superior to speech in the ordinary sense. He aims at removing the hierarchic structure altogether. Writing for him means the fundamental process of articulation and differentiation, found in both written and oral language. It is that prevocal, primordial activity of differentiation that originates language and thus bestows consciousness and gives rise to being. Hence Derrida's project of a grammatology, a science of writing, replacing semiology and overcoming the phonocentric illusion of a pure presence and the dream of a transcendental signified. Grammatology sees language as the play of differential systems and as signifying in spite of the absence of an object.

How does all this translate into a technique of interpretation? What is the deconstructive way with a text?

Deconstructive criticism is an aggregate of interpretive practices, not a unitary method. There is then no possibility of drawing up a complete list of techniques. Most noticeable perhaps is the way a deconstructive reading aims at relationships unperceived by the writer of the text. It does not simply follow the meanings as presented, but looks for what is not under the writer's control. A deconstructive reading often seizes upon what is marginal, accidental, seemingly irrelevant. It finds repressed elements that in effect undermine the text in its straightforward meaning. Repeat and undermine is the general formula. The deconstructive critics do not skip the conventional repetition of the text but carry it out minutely and laboriously. What distinguishes them is that in doing so they uncover the elements within the text that subvert its apparent meaning, rendering unstable its textual organization and its pattern of concepts. They thus question the tradition to which the text belongs.

Rather than attempting to summarize the diverse variety of critical techniques deployed by the deconstructionists, I will try to capture their fundamental approach in these few sentences: There is nothing outside of the text. There is no literal meaning. There is no metalanguage. The aim of interpretation is not truth but dissemination.

Meaning emerges from the interplay of signifiers and significations, not from a relation of reference to what is external to the text. For the interpreter there is nothing outside of the text. The free play of significations is open-ended and never halts at a stable, self-authenticating meaning; the plurality within the text never yields to the claimed finality of a literal interpretation. Every text is dependent upon other texts and thus penetrated by prior codes, concepts, and conventions. This intertextual relationship has no internal limit. Intertextuality breaks open every context as arbitrary and, if imposed, as authoritarian. There is no end to the play between text and text, so that the whole world becomes an infinite text without boundaries. There is no point from which this intertextual process can be dominated. There is no metalanguage, which stands above intertextuality. Hence the interpreter should not seek unity of meaning, a closure of play, a totalized, coherent reading, but celebrate the explosion and fragmentation of meaning and extol playfulness over rationality, dissemination over truth.

It may be summed up in this oft-quoted passage from Derrida on the two kinds of interpretation:

> There are thus two interpretations of interpretation, of structure, of sign, of play. The one seeks to decipher, dreams of deciphering a truth or an origin which escapes play and the order of the sign, and which lives the necessity of interpretation as an exile. The other, which is no longer turned toward the origin, affirms play and tries to pass beyond man and humanism, the name of man being the name of that being who, throughout the history of metaphysics or of ontotheology—in other words, throughout his entire history—has dreamed of full presence, the reassuring foundation, the origin and the end of play.[72]

Such then is the point reached in our time by the critique of metaphysics and of ontotheology.

But where does that leave us religiously and theologically? Has not my opposition to a metaphysical elaboration of mythical religion led me, if I follow Derrida, into a form of atheism and nihilism? More precisely, is not my own insistence upon the reality of transcendent love as foundational simply one more disguised vestige of metaphysics from a deconstructionist perspective? Does it not replace the endless play of representations or interpretations by an epiphany or presence of the represented?

The matter is not as clear as might at first appear. We are only at the beginnings of a theological assimilation and critique of deconstruction.

The results are not yet in. But some preliminary remarks may prevent us excluding the possibility of a *rapprochement* from the outset.

Faith has a paradoxical character. It is a presence that is at the same time an absence, because no positive experience can lay hold of the Transcendent. At the heart of faith is a negative experience, an experience that seems like a nonexperience, because it is the breakdown of every finite experience, of all our concepts, images and feelings. Faith follows a narrow path between idolatry on the one side and nihilism on the other. Much religion is idolatrous inasmuch as it absolutizes some finite experience or expression. When faith is not idolatrous, it is difficult to distinguish from nihilism, because the presence it mediates is as transcendent an absence on the human level, its plenitude is a void or emptiness of finite reality and meaning, its love coexists with a sense of abandonment. What distinguishes the negative experience of faith from the unfaith of nihilism is precisely the refusal of closure, the willingness to accept a world without boundaries, even though on the cognitive level that demands the surrender of a stable truth, a fixed center, a final meaning of our religious texts and of our human existence.

Hence the presence of faith is not the immediate presence of a luminous reality or self-authenticating truth but the presence of a hidden God in the darkness or void at the heart of human existence. The epiphany of the hidden God is a centerless repetition of successive reinterpretations, an endless play of significations, which cannot be halted by appeal to a definitive truth or final expression or by a claim to have uncovered the structure of all possible interpretations.

So I go along with Fergus Kerr when he suggests that theologians need not rush to reject the decentering of our thought advocated by Jacques Derrida. After all he remarks, theology is one science that has already lost its center through theological pluralism and may be further advanced in decentering than any other science. He goes on to say:

> Catholic Christianity as a system of meaning surely could do with considerable decentrement. In Catholic consciousness and practice it often seems as if the whole system were dependent on some principle of authority or the dogma of papal infallibility. In fact, of course, "Catholicism" is a much more amorphous and heterogeneous phenomenon than that—a ramification of concepts and customs of which one or other may become privileged in a given context, but in which none can make sense but for the interplay of all the others.[73]

I might add here that the privileged place of Jesus Christ in Christianity arises from his historical particularity or contingency; it is a mistake to make him a metaphysical origin or center.

There is for me something most attractive in the deconstructionist emphasis upon the joyous affirmation of the free play of the world, the replacement of the ironclad rationality of a Lonergan or Habermas with the notion of playfulness. As Kerr says, it "might not be so different from a joyful acceptance of the sheer gratuitousness—the 'grace'—of what is and what happens."[74] But there is also a dark element in my own consciousness. The probability that in a decade or so any of us who survive will have entered into the hell following a nuclear war makes it impossible for me to treat rationally elaborated worldviews with solemn seriousness. Our sanity is preserved in this present world not by rational argument or appeal to invariant structures but by rejoicing in the sheer unexpectedness, the ungrounded giftfulness, which characterizes the game of human existence and which might yet save us.

Myth and metaphysics! What then is still living in the mythical version of the Christian religion and in the metaphysical and doctrinal structures built upon it? Not much is left of the metaphysics, and the doctrinal elaboration needs to lose its rigidity. But what is of continuing validity in mythical Christianity is the understanding of religious language as metaphorical or poetic language and the acknowledgment that goes with this of the indispensable function of the imagination and feeling, of tradition and community. The pragmatic version of Christianity as it historically developed in the context of liberalism lost its hold upon the transcendent substance of Christian faith because of the narrowness of its view of language and reason. Hence, to assess the second, pragmatic version of Christianity, we must compare and contrast the liberal and conservative traditions of discourse.

CHAPTER 8

Liberals versus Conservatives

The interpretation of Christianity towards which I myself am reaching through the critical discussion of the four models of Christian religion belongs by its fundamental principle or generative idea to the second model or type: namely, pragmatic Christianity. That fundamental principle is the identification of Christianity not with a comprehensive worldview or with a body of doctrine, but with a practical way of life in this world. The meanings embodied in the Christian way of life are expressed in images and stories and can be partially articulated in beliefs, namely in judgments of fact and judgments of value. But the primary presence of those meanings is in concrete Christian practice. Theoretical or ideological forms of expression are derivative in relation to Christian practice and divorced from it become mere verbiage and empty gesturing. The Christian religion does not provide a self-sufficient system of ideas.

Quite apart from any reference to the Marxist view of the primacy of practice, there is a particular, religious reason for refusing to give Christian religion a theoretical center of reference or, to put it in another way, a foundation in theory. It is that Christian practice is a response to the reality of a transcendent gift; it is the living out of the concrete experience of transcendent reality. Hence Christian practice does not conform to any scale of values or set of criteria, worked out within a purely human frame of reference. In that sense it is subversive of all the orders devised by human beings for their security and prosperity; assessed by enlightened self-interest, it demands the impossible, the unreasonable; it produces the unplanned, the unexpected, the inconvenient. Christians do not suppose—or, at least, in my opinion, should not suppose—that the human situation can be significantly improved by the development of natural human capacities or by the exercise of ordinary human abilities. Christian practice is indeed a transformative principle in the world—not, however, as an achievement of human morality but as a free gift of God's love, shifting human action on to a higher level beyond mere morality. Hence the paradoxical, shocking character of the parables and sayings of Christ.

Both intellectuals and dogmatists in their respective ways commission the mind to pass judgment—as it were, from a height—upon every experience we have. For the intellectual the mind does so in virtue of its own autonomous norms. For the dogmatist conceptualized formulations, made authoritative, serve as a mental normative framework within which experience is expected to fit. Christian practice as the presence of a transcendent, redemptive principle in human affairs does not accept the supposed invulnerable autonomy and superiority of mind or submit to the limitations of fixed formulations. For the Christian the mind is as subject to sin and corruption as any other aspect of human living. When a person is not open to the gift of transcendent love, not prepared to go beyond the self to a participation in the divine, the mind becomes a tool of self-interest, and its very religious formulations are used as a protection against the disruptive impetus of the experience of Christian faith.

But am I not leaving the way open for any excess of fanaticism or religious enthusiasm and handing Christian practice over to the irrational? Well, first, religious history would seem to show that fanaticism is more likely to arise from immoderate claims to the truth of one's ideas than from an insistence upon the primacy of practice, accompanied by a modest reserve about the degree of truth possessed by any theoretical formulations. Second, my insistence upon the primacy of the Christian practice of love should not in any way be interpreted as excluding the permanent function of theoretical activity, particularly the constant need for a critique of the judgments of fact and judgments of value implicit in concrete forms of Christian practice and consequently a critique of that practice itself.

What is being rejected is not critical reflection upon practice but the epistemological approach, which interprets criticism as the search for some indubitable starting-point, some autonomous theoretical foundation or center of reference. There is no absolute starting point. Criticism is an ongoing process of reflection, in which the resolution of one set of questions or stage of thought leads to another set or stage, not in any strictly logical succession but as in a continuing conversation. Further, while theoretical activity has its own integrity, it takes place not in isolation but in a reciprocal relationship with the other activities constituting the totality of a way of life. Elements are criticized in relation to the whole, namely, the way of life, of which they are parts. The way of life will be brought into relationship with other ways of life, but again this cannot be done in a purely theoretical fashion. In brief, the effective functioning of critical reflection in its prevention of a mindless activism seems to me to be better preserved by a modesty of theoretical claims and an acknowledgment of the interaction between theoretical thought and the practical outlook and way of living of the concrete subjects of theoretical activity.

The identification of the Christian religion with the reality of a practical way of life, namely, that of transcendent love, does not therefore make Christianity an irrational enthusiasm. Indeed, such a transcendent horizon for practical living frees the mind from the biases created by self-interest or group prejudice and from the narrowness of absolutized formulations.

I am agreeing with the humanist and liberal identification of authentic Christianity with a practical way of life. I am in sympathy with those who rejected the Christian religion when it had taken the form of a fixed body of revealed doctrines and refused the heteronomous authority of a Church making absolute claims in the name of revelation. The dogmatic version of Christianity was a block to human intellectual development and the absolutist authority of the Church an obstacle to genuine human freedom. But in reaction against a reified and authoritarian form of Christianity, the humanists, deists, rationalists, and liberals lost sight of the transcendent core of Christian faith. Christianity cannot be reduced to an ethic or a natural theology. The persistence, despite the onslaught of criticism over centuries, of mythical, visionary, and mystical versions of Christian religion shows that the practical reality of Christian faith cannot in its transcendence be adequately expressed in terms of a humanist ethic or a rational theism.

Once the transcendence of Christian experience has been recognized, the indispensable function of tradition and community reemerges, even after the rejection of a doctrinalized form of tradition and of an absolutist form of Church authority. Although, sociologically speaking, the Church may take the form of a voluntary association, with the full participation of all its members in its organization and action, it is not as a community the mere free creation of its members but the effect of a transcendent presence or gift. The Christian Church in that sense is always a reality prior to its individual members, not their product. Tradition is the memory of that community and of its transcendent origin. It can never be replaced by the simple operation of reason.

The inadequacy of classical liberalism as a context for elaborating a pragmatic version of Christian religion may be made clear by contrasting the liberal and conservative traditions of discourses as these were exemplified in the nineteenth century in Bentham and Coleridge, "the two great seminal minds of England in their age," as John Stuart Mill calls them in his famous brace of essays.[75] By a tradition of discourse I mean a way of using language and all that presupposes.

Bentham's view of language is well summed up in this sentence of Mill: "Words, he thought, were perverted from their proper office when they were employed in uttering anything but precise logical truth."[76] The aim should be to make language entirely clear and precise. The phrase Bentham repeatedly used to dismiss moral speculations that did not follow his method was "vague generalities."[77] He declared that all poetry was misrepresentation, an exaggeration for effect.[78]

The high-flown obscurity of Coleridge is notorious. It was amusingly satirized in several of the novels of Thomas Love Peacock, where Coleridge appears as Mr. Moley Mystic in *Melincourt,* Mr. Flosky in *Nightmare Abbey* and Mr. Skionar in *Crotchet Castle.* Mr. Flosky remarks, "I pity the man who can see the connection of his own ideas. Still more do I pity him, the connection of whose ideas any other person can see."[79] Thus, the reputation of the "muddled Coleridgians."[80] Nevertheless, despite the obvious faults of this flawed genius, Coleridge had a rich and profound conception of language. Coulson outlines it in this fashion:

> For him [Coleridge] the primary response to language is not analytic, but fiduciary. In religion, as in poetry, we are required to make a complex act of inference and assent and we begin by taking *on trust* expressions which are usually in analogical, metaphorical, or symbolic form, and by acting out the claims they make: understanding religious language is a function of understanding poetic language.[81]

Prickett in *Romanticism and Religion* further clarifies what Coulson calls the Fiduciary Tradition of language. He writes:

> We take language and its inseparable content of ideas "on trust" because it can be accepted in no other way—any more than the mind itself can be defined from without. In contrast to Bentham and what we might call the "empirico-positivist" school of thought, Coleridge believed that in dealing with language we cannot start with the kind of definitions or premises with which we might begin some abstract problem, but we conclude by *discovering* them. Language arises not from self-evident ideas, but from the life of a particular community and culture.[82]

That way of using language may also be called poetic, inasmuch as it acknowledges the affective, nonlogical dimensions of language.

To speak of religious language is, as Prickett points out, to refer not to a way of using language, but to a particular content. Religious language, however, belongs to poetic language, first, because the poetic use of language inevitably gives rise to religious questions and, secondly, because those questions can be handled without being denatured only in poetic language, with its metaphors, symbols, and affective appeal.

We are, then, confronted with two opposing ways of using language or two traditions of discourse. The first aims at complete clarity and logical accuracy of meaning and reference. It regards metaphor as rhetorical ornament. Whatever measure of meaning symbolic language may have can, in this view, be translated into literal statements. Each individual has available the foundations of knowledge, whether as self-evident truths or sense-data. Tradition and the social community, while they may have pedagogical function, are not foundational. "Bentham failed," remarked Mill, "in deriving light from other minds.[83] According to the second view, insertion into the life and tradition of a community is foundational. Within a language accepted on trust and in communication with one another, we move towards personal insights and certainties. But the processes of our knowing are too complex and deep for explicit, logical formulation. Moreover, reality as a whole, to which language as a living principle joins us, extends beyond our clear comprehension. Metaphor, analogy, and symbol express something that can be put in no other way.

Each of the two traditions of discourse implies a different view of reason. Along with the analytic or Benthamite concept of language goes an instrumental view of reason. Reason is a tool or instrument, of the order of means not ends, to be used unilaterally by a subject to shape reality to a prior, chosen end. It enables the subject to manipulate data, concepts, and words and thus to obtain facts, so as to intervene successfully in the world and society. It is an expression of power. For the fiduciary tradition, reason is a substantive experience. It is a participation in a higher or divine principle and consequently carries within itself the structure of reality and the true order of human existence. It is thus the expression not of power but of communion among the orders of reality and the ages of history.

If I now transfer the contrast I have drawn between two traditions of discourse and of rationality to the political order, it becomes the contrast between liberal individualism and the conservative tradition, as represented preeminently by Burke.

How Bentham viewed society is made clear in this passage from Mill:

> Accordingly, Bentham's idea of the world is that of a collection of persons pursuing each his separate interest or pleasure, and prevention of whom from jostling one another more than is unavoidable, may be attempted by hopes and fears derived from three sources—the law, religion, and public opinion.[84]

The same concept of society is manifest in the incident when Coleridge said to Miss Martineau: "You seem to regard society as an aggregate of individuals." "Of course I do," she replied.[85]

Further, in liberal discourse ethics is concerned with human beings as they are, not with human beings as they should be. In other words, the classical teleological approach is rejected in favor of a scientific analysis of human factuality, together with a calculus of interests and needs.[86] Again, politics and the political order are severed from morality and religion, both of which are relegated to the private realm. Pluralism and tolerance of diverse moral and religious views, when understood within the horizon of liberal discourse, rest upon the assumption that moral and religious options are essentially private matters. The political order, with its public discourse, institutions, policies and actions, is concerned with the primary, tangible goods of life, health, and property.

In contrast to the liberal tradition, the conservative tradition rejects the narrowly instrumental view of reason and language and insists upon the indispensable function of the imagination and feeling and upon the poetic use of language. For it, political discourse remains grounded in ethics and religion. There is a stress upon tradition, understood as an organic, developing, historical process in which the past and present experiences of a community are brought together and reconciled. Because society for the conservatives is not a collection of individuals, but an historical community, great importance is assigned to order and authority and to institutions. Pluralism, with the tolerance it implies, takes the form of corporate pluralism, in which the diverse interests and beliefs represented in a society find public expression and the resulting conflict is managed and contained by an acknowledgment of the essential federalism of society. Finally, conservatives are distinguished by their keen awareness of human imperfection and sin and consequently by their suspicion of utopian schemes for the radical reform of society.

If, however, we do not confuse the conservative tradition with the reactionary or restorationist movement, we shall see that the conservatives were, like the liberals, heirs of the Enlightenment. To put it in general terms, they accepted the extension of critical rationality into the study and analysis of human society and into questions of ethics and religion. More precisely, this means, first, that they shared in the turn to the subject and were self-conscious about the limits and conditions of human knowing; second, that, although their notion of argument and data was wider and subtler, their method was broadly empirical, insofar as they considered it appropriate to argue from human experience and to ascertain the facts, historical and experiential, in dealing with the validity of social, ethical, and religious claims. The result was a concept of tradition as cumulative experience, subject therefore to change whether as development or as decline, which distinguished them from traditionalists, who understood tradition as a fixed deposit transmitted through external authority. Their outlook also reflected a recognition of the emergence of the bourgeois public sphere, what Habermas calls *Öffentlichkeit* or civil society as distinct from the State.[87] This led in discussing the political order to a shift of focus from the State to society. But, instead of the arena for the struggle of individual interests as in liberal thought, civil society was interpreted in terms of community and communicative intelligence. Coleridge argued for the formation of a religious and enlightened public, which he called the clerisy. Further, his concept of a continuing, ever-originating social contract was an expression of his ideal of a consensual, principled, constitutional political discourse. Newman, in his turn, gives the educated laity an essential function within the Church and sees them as an enlightened public, mediating the Christian faith to the political order.[88]

To conclude: As applied to Christianity, the liberal tradition led in effect to the evisceration of the Christian tradition by the removal of its transcendent core, whereas the conservative tradition made possible a transformative development. What is usually called religious liberalism belongs in fact to conservative, not to liberal, discourse and social theory.

All the same, while I recognize the negative historical experience of liberal Christianity, I still want to defend an essentially liberal, not conservative, version of Christian religion as the path to the future. My chosen interpretation remains basically liberal in its refusal of a prior, comprehensive, normative order. Despite the skillful rearguard action of the conservatives, the attempt to combine critical rationality with the mythical certitude in a prior universal order is in my opinion doomed to failure. Hence I agree with the liberal option for a plurality of orders, all existing in mutual toleration because grounded practically not theoretically. This excludes any theoretical center of reference, any foundation in theory, any indubitable or absolute starting point. Human knowledge for the liberal is fragmentary; as critically validated, it cannot give more than knowledge of the elements, it cannot give knowledge of the whole. The liberal rejects speculative reason with its claim to originate world views and metaphysical systems and opts for a critical reason that provides a rational critique of the elements of an always fragmentary knowledge. In the Christian context the liberal, unlike the conservative, refuses both the dogmatic claim to an immutable body of revealed doctrines and the ecclesiastical claim to a divinely appointed hierarchy.

Nevertheless I would argue for the possibility and the necessity of assimilating into the liberal, pragmatic option the conservative acknowledgment of the transcendent dimension of Christian practice and the consequent indispensable function of tradition and community. This implies a rejection of liberal rationalism and individualism, a rejection which will be reflected in a richer and more profound concept of language. This modified or postliberal version of pragmatic Christianity remains open to insights embodied in the mythical, visionary, and mystical versions of Christian religion.

CHAPTER 9

Natural Supernaturalism

In her commentary on Dante, Dorothy Sayers remarks, "it is the weakness of Humanism to fall short in the imagination of ecstasy."[89] Etymologically, "ecstasy" means "a standing outside of," and human beings have to stand outside of themselves, outside of this present world, which means outside the ordered framework of everyday existence, if they are to take the full measure of human life as it actually is. Many people would willingly give up the ecstasy for a moderate, balanced happiness in this world. They do not understand why men and women cannot be content with achieving a decent, virtuous life under the dictates of reason. Human beings should live together in peace, gradually moving towards a juster social order and settling their disputes by reasonable negotiation. To speak of ecstasy or eternal bliss or transcendent love is for them to promise too much and to introduce a disruptive element into the balance of human history. Forego the ecstasy as a childish illusion and accept the limitations of human existence in order to enjoy its real, though finite, possibilities.

The difficulty with the appeal to simple decency and reasonableness is that it is an appeal to what is not available if we are to judge from the facts of human history and the unending stream of evidence from present human behavior. As Dostoyevsky pointed out in *Notes from Underground,* human beings take a perverse delight in acting against reason, indeed against their own advantage. There is no possibility of flattening out the heights and depths of human existence. The call to ecstasy is an inescapable part of what it means to be human. Refuse or repress it and human life does not become calmly reasonable or respectably virtuous but diabolically evil.

Even religion in its mythical form does not do full justice to the wild, disruptive desire of human beings for rapturous bliss or to its perverse counterpart in an irrational, destructive delight in evildoing. The mythical establishment of a comprehensive, normative order, while it gives symbolic expression to the transcendent, also tends to domesticate it. John Dominic Crossan[90] makes the same point in drawing a contrast between myth and parable. Myth, he says, establishes world, parable subverts world. In other words, myths are agents of stability inasmuch as they construct a world in which we can live. But a constant temptation is to forget the limitations of every world. Hence the need for parable. Parable is a story deliberately calculated to show the limitations of myth and to shatter the world it creates, revealing the relativity of its classifications and laws.

Parable, however, provides no resting place. As subversive stories, reversing our priorities, upsetting our expectations, shattering the world in which we enclose ourselves, parables have a permanent function. But, as Crossan himself admits, we cannot live in parable alone. He says we must live in the tension between myth and parable. But here I want to insert the visionary type of Christianity, with its distinction of two worlds and its allegorical evocation of a transcendent world to come, now present by anticipation in the elect.

The governing idea of visionary Christianity is the distinction of two worlds: the present, visible world of sin and corruption and a future, hidden world of grace and glory. The distinction of two worlds, which contrasts with the single, total order of mythical religion, brings the transcendent character of human destiny into relief. It accounts for ecstasy, because the other world stands outside of the present, everyday world. It allows for the excesses of human evil, because this world is a world of sin and corruption, which will be destroyed to give place to new heavens and a new earth. Moreover, since the new order for which it hopes is not identified with the existing order but stands outside it as future—or at least as a hidden, still to be revealed possibility—the hope for it can be shared by those who in the present world are weak, powerless, and oppressed.

What, then, has visionary Christianity to offer in the present situation? How far is it a viable model today of the Christian religion?

Perhaps no feature of Christian religion has been more fiercely condemned in modern times than its dualism of two worlds and its consequent otherworldliness, namely, its indifference to this world in favor of a world to come. There are good reasons for the condemnation. The other world, conceived individualistically as the world into which each person enters at death, has been interpreted as a mere rectification of the injustices and other evils of this life. It has served as a compensatory mechanism, redistributing rewards and punishments so as to counterbalance the unjust distribution of this world. The world to come in that interpretation becomes the wishful counterpart of this world; it is like the fantasy of a poor man that he has suddenly become rich.

This form of Christianity is, I think, quite dead. Even traditional-minded Christians hesitate over their belief in personal immortality, because they are afraid of its becoming an escape from the reality of their life in this world, and they know enough psychology to make them want to avoid illusion. In other words, there is a practical sense that genuine hope for this world or the next must be grounded in actual experience. The reality constituting the world to come or life after death must be a reality manifest and operative here and now in this present world, even if we still await its consummation or final revelation.

To put it in another way, what may be called the otherworldly interpretation of the Christian dualism of two worlds, while it replaces this world in some imagined future, leaves this world in place here and now. The transformative effect of Christianity upon this world is lost by the disengagement of the promised new world from the events and actions of the course of human history. This world goes on as before, and the other world is put apart in heaven or on the other side of the end of history.

That, however, is a decadent interpretation of visionary Christianity. The sounder interpretation sees the two worlds as closely interrelated, so that the new world emerges as the transformation or destruction of the old. Whether the transformation or the destruction of the world is stressed, the new world arises like a phoenix only from the ashes of the old. It does not exist in a realm apart. The emergence of the new is the fate of the old. We cannot, therefore, disregard the old and treat it with indifference.

Such is the apocalyptic version of visionary Christianity. If otherworldy dualism is dead, there has, in contrast, been a revival of apocalypticism. Christian apocalyptic hope, fostering the expectation of nothing less than the overthrow of the existing order and the establishment of a new and lasting order, corresponds religiously to the social and political radicalism which has taken possession of the minds and hearts of many since the example of the French Revolution made fundamental changes in the order of society seem a practical possibility. Likewise, the intensity of apocalyptic hope, creating an excited sense of imminent deliverance, is the religious counterpart of the revolutionary mentality and easily merges with it. Hence Christians who in the living out of their Christian love have been led to identify themselves with the struggle of the poor and oppressed frequently express their Christian hope in terms that derive from apocalyptic. Moreover, apocalyptic conceives change as taking place through catastrophe, that is, through a sudden, violent turn of events, rather than through a process of development or evolutionary amelioration. The extreme and violent character of oppression in some countries, together with the seeming impossibility of wresting power from the oppressors by peaceful, gradual reform, makes apocalyptic appear as the only credible form of hope.

In assessing apocalyptic themes in present-day Christianity, let me begin with the phrase "natural supernaturalism," which I have taken from M.H. Abrams, who, I presume, took it from Carlyle's *Sartor Resartus*. I use it as the heading of this critique of visionary Christianity.

Abrams uses the phrase as the title of a book on tradition and revolution in Romantic literature.[91] For him Romantic thinking and imagination was a secular version of apocalyptic thinking and imagination.[92] "Natural supernaturalism" succinctly states that Romantic thought—and I would add radical thought in general—is an attempt to naturalize an originally supernatural hope. As Abrams explains, there emerged the concept of a total revolution which in a cleansing explosion of violence and destruction would reconstitute the existing political, social, and moral order from its foundations. The revolution, led by a militant élite, would in a remarkably short time change the present evil era into a lasting era of peace, justice, and general happiness.[93] Later, in contrasting that modern secular conception with its theological precedents, Abrams distinguishes apocalypse by revelation, apocalypse by revolution, and apocalypse by imagination or cognition. The high, Romantic argument was that "the mind of man confronts the old heaven and earth and possesses within itself the power, if it will but recognize and avail itself of the power, to transform them into a new heaven and new earth, by means of a total revolution of consciousness."[94]

What has moved to the forefront today is again apocalypse by revolution. The Romantic apocalypse by imagination and cognition, that is, by a total change of consciousness, has fallen victim to the widespread acceptance of Marx's contention that consciousness is not autonomous, but shaped by the concrete conditions of human social existence. But whether the cardinal change is a revolution of consciousness or a social and political revolution, what "natural supernaturalism" envisions as a possibility within human, historical attainment is the overthrow of the existing evil order and the establishment of a fundamentally new and lasting order of freedom, justice, and peace. This, in my estimation, is an illusion, an attempt by human beings to appropriate transcendence for themselves, for their own historical, finite existence. It is an attempt which generates demonic forms of pseudotranscendence.

The crux of the objection to secular apocalyptic does not lie in its placing the immediate source of the power to establish the new order in human beings and human action. To do so need not imply any denial of transcendence. Many revolutionaries or Romantics did see themselves as agents or vehicles of a force greater than themselves. Admittedly that force might be conceived as totally immanent in world process as Idea or as History, in a manner incompatible with true transcendence. But immanence need not exclude transcendence, as it does not in the doctrine of the Incarnation. The divine action may manifest itself as immanent in human action rather than as an alternative to it or as a complement alongside of it. The contrast between apocalypse by revelation and apocalypse by revolution is misleading here. It is perfectly possible to see a revolution as a revelation of God's action through the mediation of human action. Indeed, if we are to avoid a crude literalism in our understanding of divine revelation, we must allow that any such revelation is mediated through the events of human history as resulting from the action of human agents, granted that the results are in great measure unforeseen by the human agents themselves. The point, however, remains that there is no logical reason why Christians working to transform the present order radically by revolutionary action should not see themselves as instruments of a divine apocalypse, so that their active engagement in the revolutionary struggle in no way implies an assertion that their own unaided action can achieve the establishment of the new order.

What is objected to is not as such the claim to be the possessor or vehicle of revolutionary power but the conception of the result of that power. It is the secularization of the object of hope which attempts to domesticate and thus loses that transcendence in relation to which human existence should be lived. Bluntly, it is a mistake to invoke any Christian sanction for the supposition that the social, political, or personal conditions of human existence can be radically changed or that a lasting ideal order can ever be established within the framework of human history.

The concept of a final, lasting ideal order within history is incoherent. Suppose that through some cleansing upheaval or series of catastrophic changes an ideal order was established for the postrevolutionary future generations. As a finite historical order it would still be subject to change. Human existence as we know it is a process of continuous change. Since the order is by definition already ideal, any change would be for the worse. Historical change would become a process of decadence and disintegration. Further, no such ideal social and political order can serve as an answer to the problem of the human condition, because it provides "salvation" only for the generation of successful revolutionaries and for the happy postrevolutionary generations before the decline and fall of the new order. Religious hope, such as the Christian expectation of the Kingdom of God, measures up to the negativities of the human condition by including past generations within its scope, the dead as well as the living. Christian hope places its fulfilment the other side of death, in a resurrection, not in a revolution. However that might be interpreted, it is at least clear that any social and political changes this side of death, namely, within history, have only a relative importance and of themselves leave human hope unfulfilled.

What must be stressed here is that apocalyptic imagery is allegorical. In other words, it attempts to depict the ultimate victory of good over evil by imagining a divine overthrow of a known oppressive, persecuting regime. Hence the allusions to the contemporary social and political situation, intermingled with images of cosmic catastrophe, resurrection of the dead, and final divine judgment. Fundamentally, we are dealing with an allegorical expression in terms of catastrophic change in this world of what in itself defies any literal description and lies outside of time and history, namely, the definitive triumph of good over evil and the consequent fulfillment of human hope that love, goodness, and virtue are stronger than evil and will have the last word.

The persistence of millenarianism down the centuries shows the pull there is to take apocalyptic allegory literally. Millenarianism originated as an attempt to combine the hope of a heavenly, transcendent Kingdom beyond history with the hope of a fulfilment on this earth. Taking its cue from a text (20:3–6) in the Book of Revelation, it combined the two by supposing a millennium, or terrestrial reign of a thousand years by Christ, prior to the inauguration of the final Kingdom. In the course of time, millenarianism became, more loosely, the expectation of a messianic kingdom to be realized in some fashion here on this earth. Such an expectation is a harmful delusion. Apocalyptic imagery, it bears repeating, is an allegorical presentation of an ultimate fulfilment which cannot be identified with any conceivable social and political order here on this earth. Its function is precisely to image forth and insist upon the transcendent grounds for our hope in the midst of persecution, worldly disaster, and the earthly triumph of the oppressors.

Are we back, then, to the otherworldly dualism, previously rejected? What can we hope for on this earth? Let me take the second question first.

Those who hope and work for a radical change in the existing social and political situation often assign some root cause of our present ills. Thus, many denounce capitalism as the source of present social evils and argue that socialism or the abolition of private ownership of the means of production would bring a new order of justice and freedom. Feminists, on their part, regard patriarchy as the deeper disorder and contend that the full emancipation of women is what would transform the present order from the ground upwards and usher in a new era. No doubt there are other conceivable hypotheses. Now there is no reason why a Christian should not adhere to one or other of them. The Christian faith does not provide any ready-made answers to questions of social, political, and cultural analysis, but at the same time it does not exclude the possibility of a general human advance through the solution of a major problem or the removal of a major evil.

There are propositions in the corpus of the Christian tradition, especially propositions formulating judgments of value, which are relevant to any analysis of the present situation and choice of a course of action. For example, a Christian may excuse or regard as inevitable the exploitative features of capitalism, but no Christian can consistently justify that exploitation or take profitability as an end overriding considerations of justice. Further, a Christian in assessing the present concrete situation and surveying the options available may come to the conclusion that socialism is the only political stance actually compatible with

Christian values and may advocate Christian socialism. Other Christians may argue that capitalism, especially in view of the threat of atheistic communism, is the most acceptable economic system, as creating the best opportunity for the social and political realization of Christian values. And so on. The point I want to make is that no overall judgment concerning the present situation and future possibilities will be so evidently bound up with Christian beliefs and values as to impose itself upon all sincere Christians. Christian values are certainly relevant in choosing among the available social and political options or in opening up new choices. There are policies, such as apartheid in South Africa, which evidently and beyond any unprejudiced denial contradict those values. Generally speaking, however, Christian values are relevant without determining the issue, because of the complex factual judgments involved and the conflict of values found in any concrete situation. Christians must work with others towards a gradual clarification and partial, though ever widening, consensus.

In brief, what Christians, like others, may hope for on this earth is an actualization of the possibilities in the concrete situation and therefore a greater fulfillment of human potential than is at present the case. As to the direction, means, and feasibility of social and political progress, Christians will differ among themselves as well as from others. With their fellow Christians and with others, they must enter into that public debate which should constitute political life. In that context, Christian faith has both conservative and radical effects.

It moves Christians towards conservative options inasmuch as it leads them to uncover as repressed or pseudoreligion the pursuit of a final, lasting ideal order here on earth. For Christians the struggle between good and evil, between sin and love of God, will continue until history comes to an end in the Last Judgment. Redemption from the basic negatives of the human condition—guilt, failure, suffering, death—is to be found only in a transcendent communion, which embraces the human race as a whole, the dead as well as the living, not just the beneficiaries of a temporal, political revolution. Since from a Christian perspective every social and political order is imperfect, of limited value, and inevitably transient, constantly threatened in its positive values by human sinfulness, their Christian faith creates a hesitancy over destroying any existing order in the hope of replacing it by a better. Christians will often take a conservative stance because of their awareness that the embodiment of moral and religious values in human institutions is difficult and any achievement always ambiguous and precarious.

That conservative thrust is, however, counterbalanced by a Christian radicalism. This stems from the relativizing of every historical order and at the same time from an unshakable assurance about the possibilities of humanity under grace, an assurance preventing any lapse into cynicism or despair. Christian faith is essentially subversive in its refusal to canonize any existing state of affairs, its resistance to the absolutizing of any institution, including religious institutions, and its openness to change. In placing their ultimate hope in a transcendent order, Christians are made radically free in relation to any and every establishment. For that reason, visionary Christianity, which as a symbol system highlights the radical elements in Christianity, finds its strongest embodiment in dissenting groups and is resistant to the integration of Christian institutions into the dominant social and political order.

The source of Christian radicalism is the lived experience of transcendent love. The reality of Christian love as experienced in the practice of that love opens individuals and communities to a longing beyond any earthly or limited fulfilment and at the same time moves people to love others in an unrestricted fashion that rejects any confinement within the many boundaries, such as race, sex, class, set up to protect the enclosed self of those who refuse ecstasy. The love is ecstatic, not in the narrow, mystical sense of producing an altered state of consciousness, but for two reasons. First, it moves the person to transcend or stand outside of all the distinctions of wealth, power, education, or fortune inevitable in any political or social order. Second, that movement comes from living in the joyful tension and unrest of an openness to the Infinite.

It is at this point we can see why a refusal to identify the object of Christian hope with some future ideal social and political order does not force us back into a decadent otherworldly dualism. Eternal life is not a new and different life, awaiting us in heaven and compensating us for the meaningless misery of this present existence. Eternal life is a present reality, essentially the reality of transcendent love. Admittedly, before death and in history this life is lived under conditions different from those, beyond our conception, which lie the other side of death and history. But the life is essentially the same, and already the reality of transcendent love is a transformative principle, giving present meaning and fulfilment to those still in the midst of the ills of historical existence. Those who witness to that love in poverty, suffering, weakness, oppression, and persecution are not declared happy because they will receive a compensatory reward but because they are in reality here and now significantly more fulfilled or blessed than those who enjoy worldly wealth and power without the transcendent love, which is the one thing essential.

At the same time, because transcendent love is a principle transformative of human life and human action, it is always operative according to the degree of its presence. Even though it looks beyond history for the final fulfilment of its hope, it does not allow a passive waiting for the final end, whatever some Christian visionaries have erroneously thought from the time of St. Paul onward. The general attitude it inculcates may be deduced from the Christian response to physical suffering. While Christians do not believe that physical suffering can be eliminated in this world, their Christian love leads them to do their utmost to relieve the suffering of others. The same applies to social injustice and oppression. Though Christians do not place their hope in the achievement of an ideal, historical order, their love should be ceaselessly operative for the removal of injustice and the relief of oppression beyond any criterion of success as the world measures it.

The extreme, seemingly excessive character of the apocalyptic imagery of cosmic catastrophe and divine intervention is an attempt to express the persistence of active hope when from a worldly standpoint the situation is hopeless, so that any hope for change or liberation is apparently hope for the impossible. As Christian Love is ecstatic in its transcendence, so Christian hope is ecstatic in its hope for the impossible. But that is mere talk unless the actual presence of Christian love and hope is operative as a transformative force here and now.

A few remarks may be added concerning the present use of apocalyptic imagery.

The theme of the quest, with Jesus as the victorious hero, journeying through death to resurrection and new life, with his disciples following after him, is still valid and effective in its use of archetypal material. The presentation, however, of human history as a struggle between the children of light and the children of darkness is dangerous and has proved harmful more than once in the past. The danger lies in the constant temptation to identify the children of light and the children of darkness with two actual groups of people—with two States or two nations or two classes or two religious bodies. The apocalyptic struggle between the forces of good and the forces of evil takes place in reality within each individual and each community of whatever kind. Its depiction as a warfare between two armies of people is symbolic. The absoluteness of the opposition between good and evil as such cannot be transferred to the opposition between any two concrete groups of human beings. Even the opposition between sinners and the just, or between believers and unbelievers, is not an absolute one within history. Sinners may be converted and are not utterly sinful; the just may fall away and are never wholly just. Apocalyptic imagery may make us forget the confusion and ambiguity that marks the moral and religious life of human beings within history. It tempts us to project the evil found throughout humankind upon a particular group of people, upon our political or religious enemies, with deplorable, indeed sometimes horrifying results.

There is another dangerous feature in apocalyptic imagery. It is the theme of violent, catastrophic destruction as a cleansing renewal of the earth or as the pangs of the birth of a new order. Nuclear extermination has now stepped into place as the acme of physical power and the extremity of violence. Surely this should make us question the appropriateness of the easy and frequent use in the Bible, especially in the Psalms and apocalyptic passages, of violence as the symbolic depiction of the divine saving power. After all, we are confronted in actual reality with the imminent threat of a black apocalypse, namely, a meaningless destruction, which will not cleanse or purify the earth but irremediably pollute it, which will not open the way to a better future but close off human history from any future. Some would argue that this threat excludes any use of violence as an instrument of social and political policy, because once recourse is had to violence, nothing in principle limits its escalation to the extreme of coercive power available. However, without raising here the question whether a policy of nonviolence is now in all circumstances the only reasonable one, we may still think that the religious use of the imagery of violence as the manifestation of God is now to be avoided as obsolete and as apt to arouse dangerous emotions. When apocalyptic is correctly interpreted, the emphasis falls on the coming of the new order, not on the destruction of the old. The old is shattered because the new comes into being. We need to develop an imagery of wondrous transformation, rather than of destructive conquest to express the ultimate triumph of grace.

To sum up: Those who like myself interpret Christianity primarily as a practice or way of life and thus ally ourselves with the pragmatic form of Christian faith cannot without loss and distortion pass over the contribution of visionary or apocalyptic Christianity. That contribution is to the effect that Christian faith is a genuinely new life, that it is not to be reduced to the limits of any mere humanism, that it is ecstatic in its call to rapturous bliss and transcendent love. Christianity is not a moralism; it is a practice beyond human measure, grounded in a vision of foolish love and impossible hope.

CHAPTER 10

The Retreat into Privacy

The fourth model of the Christian religion is the mystical. What contributions has mystical Christianity to make to the task of keeping Christian faith as a live option in the present situation? Does it, as a particular form or type of Christian faith, bring any distortions or imbalances with it?

Mystical Christianity gives explicit expression to two fundamental insights which, at least implicitly, must be part of all genuine Christian faith.

The first insight is that Christian faith, hope, and love have unknown mystery as their term and do not have an object, namely a referent which can be grasped and formulated. God is not an object which can be apprehended conceptually by human intelligence, even when illumined by faith. God's transcendence prevents that. Hence all our concepts of God are symbolic constructs, which contain no proper knowledge of God, no knowledge of God as God is in the divine self. Christian faith does indeed have a real referent distinct from the consciousness of the subject. Faith is not enclosed upon the subject; it is not a consciousness simply of our own subjective state. The consciousness is not of the self but of God. There is, then, an experience of God, but God is experienced as an inapprehensible and ineffable reality at the term of a limitless longing and love, a reality drawing us and real beyond measure in the power and sweetness of that drawing, but all the while remaining hidden, not coming within our grasp as an object of knowledge. Therefore, as the anonymous author of the fourteenth-century *Cloud of Unknowing* says, God may be reached by love, but not by thought.[95]

Since all genuine faith relates to God as transcendent, it must recognize that it cannot make God an object and that to identify God with any of its images or concepts is idolatry. There is for that reason a mystical core in all faith. However, while nonmystical forms of Christian religion, especially the mythical type, stress the positive function of religious images and concepts, the mystical underlines their limitations.

That difference of emphasis becomes much more acute with the second fundamental insight embodied in mystical Christianity, namely, the ultimate inadequacy of all language to express religious truth. That insight relativizes all religious systems, doctrines, institutions, and practices to an extent that troubles and provokes resistance from those who take their stand upon the exclusive truth of some orthodoxy or traditional system. What may be called the mystical principle is the equivalence of symbols. Since the limitless term of mystical experience lies beyond conceptual knowledge and is reached and expressed only indirectly through symbols, many different symbols and symbolic systems can function in that indirect fashion. The truth and efficacy of one symbolic system does not exclude the truth and efficacy of other, different systems. For that reason mysticism from the nineteenth century onwards has proved a popular resort for interpreting the plurality of world religions.

The principle of the equivalence of symbols helps us to reconcile the particularity of every mystical experience in the concrete with the unity, so often claimed, of all mystical experience. The immediacy of mystical experience is a mediated immediacy. There is indeed an immediacy in as much as the movement of mystical ascent passes beyond all images, concepts, techniques, practices to a direct experience of the Godhead. Nevertheless, that ascent takes place only in the context of a particular tradition and through the use of its particular fund of interpretations and expressions—in brief, through a particular language. According to the tradition to which he or she belongs, the mystic follows a particularly conceived path to a particularly conceived goal. At the same time, the immediacy of the experience reached, its surpassing of every formulation, its relativizing of every interpretation, including its own, grounds the recognition that there are other paths and that differently conceived goals may be ways of pointing to a single ineffable experience with a single ineffable referent or term.

There is a debate among scholars whether mystical experience is one or many and whether it is reducible to a few types and, if so, to which types.[96] To enter into the debate in detail is beyond my present purpose. Enough to say, I acknowledge the need to insist upon the diversity and particularity of mystical experience in the concrete, against both the too easy and sweeping assertion of the unity of mystical experience and the use of inadequate typologies. All the same, the principle of the equivalence of symbols, with the opening out it implies from particularity to universality, is an undoubted feature of mysticism and is the reason for the well-known tension between mysticism and orthodoxy in more than one religious tradition. At any rate, it explains the affinity Troeltsch, as I have already noted, discerned between modern thought and mysticism, when he set forth his threefold typology of the sociological development of Christian thought, namely, Church, sect, and mysticism. It was the mystical principle that enabled modern thinkers to overcome the exclusive particularity of a supernaturally instituted Christian religion and to interpret Christian religious experience in the context of the unity in pluralism of the religious history of humankind.

Within the mystical type of religion, however, the insight that all religious language is inadequate may go beyond the relativizing recognition of plurality. It may embody a conviction of the ultimate inadequacy of any human attempt to make sense of the chaos, confusion, and meaninglessness of life in this world. It is not that religious language is so far inadequate that recourse must be had to a multiplicity of symbols but that there is no way in thought, theoretical or symbolic, through the aporias of human existence. We do not have answers capable of satisfying our thought; we have only the reality of a practice of love. It is the lived experience of that love which is expressed in religious symbols and which gives rise to various formulations of the human condition, of human possibilities, and of human destiny. But these formulations should not be taken as if they were theoretically grounded explanatory accounts. They represent the play of human desire, a desire grounded in the experience of love and hope. The satirical thrust in mystical religion, which pours scorn upon the absurdity of any absolutist religious claims, brings a needed check to the ambitions of the religious consciousness. I see, therefore, the positive contribution of mystical religion as capable of incorporation into a basically pragmatic type of Christianity. Its insight 1) that Christian faith confronts mystery, 2) that this compels one to find the universal in the particular and to move from exclusiveness to pluralism, and 3) that we have to live in love and hope but without answers, is an enlargement of our understanding of Christian religion as a way of life in the practice of love. Thus, mystical Christianity, like visionary Christianity can, at least in part, serve as a complement to pragmatic Christianity.

Of itself, however, it produces a one-sidedness, which calls for critical attention. The source of the imbalance is the tendency to identify the interior self with the private self.

By the interior self I mean the conscious subject as distinctly aware of his or her individual being and activity. The interior self is the self-reflective self, the self as a self-aware subject, constituting an interior world over against the external world. It is the interior self that is the subject of the mystical ascent, even if the interpretation favoured is that at its deepest core the individual self is one without distinction with Ultimate Reality, so that individual self is not a substantial or permanent reality. We speak of the interior self as soon as a differentiation of consciousness has brought a reflective distinction between the world of the conscious self and the world of society and nature.

The private self is the self taken as limited to the private sphere of individual and family life. It is a twofold limitation. First, the object of concern and the aims and values pursued are not taken beyond the individual self and the personal development and intimate, interpersonal relationships of that self. Or, to put it negatively, social and political affairs are considered as not being an essential concern of the interior or spiritual life. Second, the interior self when made private operates as if independent of social and political factors and as though the subject's action and development were dependent exclusively upon the interior factors of individual consciousness. The path of contemplation is understood as isolated from social and political influences.

In brief, mystical religion unless corrected encourages a privatization of religion, which identifies the religious life with an exclusive concern for the development of the interior life of the individual self and which remains unaware of the social and political factors that set objective limits to what can be achieved within the sphere of individual consciousness. There is no doubt that the recurrent upsurges of interest in mystical religion are linked to a sense of powerlessness in relation to the social and political situation and thus represent a flight from the objectified structures and institutionalized power of society into the freedom of a disengaged consciousness.

Nevertheless there is no necessary contradiction between mystical religion and full social and political involvement, nor between mystical religion and an acknowledgment of the limits set by social and political factors to any development of individual consciousness. The interior self, the subject of the mystical ascent, is indeed from one standpoint asocial and apolitical, because the openness to the transcendent, the orientation towards absolute mystery, prevents that self from being enclosed within the finitude and relativity of any social and political order. But from another standpoint the interior self is the very source and ground of any mature social involvement and political participation, because individual self-awareness releases the person into freedom and responsibility. Genuine politics, as distinct from conformity to the demands of an impersonal, bureaucratic system or submission to domination by a ruling group or monarch, requires the responsible self. To become a responsible self, the human subject must retain an indefeasibly private core, and this is what is secured by the mystical openness of the self to the transcendent.

That the mystic is prepared for social and political action rather than permanently withdrawn from society and politics has long been recognized and is confirmed by the personal history of quite a few mystics. What is less recognized is that the techniques of mystical contemplation and the resulting stages of contemplative consciousness are conditioned by their social context. Without presupposing any iron determinism, we do need more detailed sociological studies linking the various manifestations of mystical consciousness with social causes and pressures.

To do justice to the positive contribution of mystical Christianity and to check its anarchistic or privatizing tendencies, a new concept of the Church is called for. The struggle in the context of the modern world for such a new concept may be related to the account given by Habermas of the emergence of the bourgeois public.[97]

The bourgeois public sphere or public arose as a new historical reality in the seventeenth century in England and in the eighteenth century in France. Its context was the development in modern society of a distinction between the public power of the State and the private sphere of civil society. That distinction between public and private spheres was unknown in medieval society. The medievals had the concept of representative publicness, such as was embodied in secular rulers or kings and ecclesiastical rulers or bishops. Representative publicness was the public representation of dominion or power, but it did not form a social sphere over against another, private social sphere. The distinction between two social spheres, one public, one private, came when the State developed an extensive bureaucratic administration. A distinction was created between all that came under the administrative organization or public power of the State and what was left free for private initiative and control. The latter, which with the emergence of economic liberalism included industry and commerce, was of social relevance and constituted civil society as distinct from the State.

The bourgeois critical public arose within the context of civil society. It related private individuals or autonomous subjects politically. It did not relate them as business associates, because as business associates they were each pursuing their private affairs. Nor did it relate them as participating in the legal structure of society, because as legal participants they were related to the public power of the State. Individual citizens formed a critical public when in virtue of the freedom of association, freedom of assembly, and freedom of speech they came together to discuss matters of general interest, particularly those concerned with the conduct of the public power of the State. In other words, the bourgeois critical public exercised a political power distinct from that of the State by means of publicity, that is, by a critique, control, and surveillance through public discourse of the authority of the State.

The emergence of the bourgeois public marks a change in the very conception of authority. Previously when new groups succeeded in gaining political power or existing ruling groups increased their share of power, the new positions were established by an altered distribution of rights and privileges. But the bourgeois public was not as such a new division of public power. It consisted of private citizens who did not as such rule or exercise a function in the public power of the State. The principle behind the bourgeois public was that all authority was subject to critique, control, and surveillance through open discourse, free from constraint. This implied a change in the nature of authority, a transformation of traditional authority into rational authority. The idea of authority as being at least in some final instance beyond critique or control is rejected. All authority is rational as being without limitation or exception subject to the demand to justify its claims and its action rationally before a critical public.

Before relating the concept of the public to the changing concept of the Church, we must first notice that, according to Habermas, the evolution of the capitalist economy has led to the disintegration of the bourgeois public. Control by the large corporations has removed key issues of general interest from public discussion. The movement of society in the direction of technocracy, in which public decisions are legitimated by an appeal to experts, has been accompanied by a depoliticization of the public sphere. Public opinion is no longer the product of rational argumentation and critical reflection but the result of manipulation. The aim of commercial advertising and of political propaganda in the late capitalist society is to prevent the formation of a critical public.

The contrast between the old and new meanings of public opinion may be seen by comparing the working of the medium of the printed word (book, pamphlet, or newspaper) with that of the new mass media of radio, television, and film, particularly that of television. The printed word allowed the reader to establish a critical distance from what was written, to go back over it, and to contradict it. It also led to the formation of a public engaged in rational discussion of what they had read. Television, in contrast, by its immediacy and fleetingness inhibits the creation of a critical distance with the ability to contradict or discuss what is said or shown. Moreover, individuals are addressed directly in the privacy of their homes. That situation does not lead to the creation of groups engaged in public discussion. Instead of a critical public, there is a mass audience, open in its passivity to manipulation.

But for present problems to be adequately met, the Churches must first assimilate the valid insights of the earlier period. How in fact did the Churches relate themselves to the newly emergent critical public?

The Catholic Church resisted it. It refused the application of public critique, control, and surveillance to its own traditional authority. It rejected the implication of a critical public, namely, that sovereignty or authority rested upon consensus. De Maistre gave an extreme expression of the Catholic position, but what he stated was not significantly different from the later teaching of Pius IX, who explicitly rejected the modern freedoms that constituted the bourgeois public or from the dominant ultramontane theology. De Maistre identified sovereignty with infallibility. The authority of the Church was beyond reason and dispute. The Church did not enter into argument. Its decisions must be accepted without question. That is why De Maistre became a political theorist, not a theologian. Christian teaching was not subject to argument; it had simply to be stated to call for acceptance.[98] The official Catholic Church has not even yet unambiguously accepted the transformation of authority implied by recognition of a critical public.

We shall see in a moment the move by some Catholics towards a new conception of the Church. But let me immediately mention the clearest contribution to the political question of sovereignty. It came from Newman. Harold Laski calls Newman's *Letter to the Duke of Norfolk* "as perhaps the profoundest discussion of the nature of obedience and of sovereignty to be found in the English language."[99] Newman was answering the contention of Gladstone that, because of the Vatican Council's definition of papal supremacy and infallibility, no British subject could be both loyal to the Crown and a Catholic. Newman, while acknowledging the papacy as the supreme ecclesiastical authority, rejected what David Nicholls calls moral sovereignty, namely, the claim to an authority to which obedience is due whatever it wills, a body whose commands are morally binding in all circumstances.[100] Newman writes: ". . . if either the Pope or the Queen demanded of me an 'Absolute Obedience,' he or she would be transgressing the laws of human nature and human society. I give an absolute obedience to neither."[101] His famous conclusion was: "If I am obliged to bring religion into after-dinner toasts (which indeed does not seem quite the thing), I shall drink—to the Pope if you please—still to Conscience first, and to the Pope afterwards."[102] Laski, with some reason, doubts whether Newman's attitude represented with any accuracy the policy of Rome. Rome, it would seem, even after the Second Vatican Council has continued to claim moral sovereignty.

The relation of the bourgeois critical public to Protestant theology is more complicated. In an earlier essay,[103] I related Protestant theology to three stages in the history of the bourgeois public. The first stage in that history was the struggle with absolutist power and with the social system of the estates. The second stage was the coming into power of the bourgeois public in the nineteenth century. The third stage was its decline and its conflict with new forms of social organization.

The first stage corresponds to the *Aufklärung* theology of Semler (1725–91). Semler made a distinction between public and private religion. The public religion had dogmas and creeds, church rituals and preaching. Private religion was built upon free insight. "Private" here means the free, independent enquiry and insight of mature Christians. Corresponding to the distinction between public religion and private religion is a distinction between a public official theology and a private theology. The rational meaning of the institution with its public religion and theology is to be the school of Christianity, but a school is not the whole of life. Alongside the institution is an autonomous and free Christianity. Semler wished to limit the power and function of the Church in the way in which the bourgeois public endeavoured to limit the power and function of the State.

It is to the beginning of the second stage, the stage of the coming to power of the bourgeois public that Schleiermacher's theology and Hegel's philosophy of religion belong. The critique of the dogmatic form of the Christian tradition is now taken for granted; the point now is to develop its doctrinal content in a free and independent fashion. This is bourgeois society bringing Christian culture under its principle of freedom. While Schleiermacher fits comfortably here, Hegel does not, because of his incorporation of the Church into the State and his insistence upon the unified nation-State as the embodiment of Reason.

The third stage in the history of the bourgeois public sphere or civil society is the time of its decline. Corresponding to this stage was the crushing of the theology of the *Aufklärung* and of the Romantic renaissance by the two extremes of the restoration of dogmatic and exclusive Church Christianity on the one hand and the radical critique of religion by the Young Hegelians on the other. Both extremes had in common the rejection of the bringing together of the Christian tradition and modern subjectivity and freedom, which had been achieved in the early phase of nineteenth-century theology.

Let me at this point try to formulate the problem at issue more precisely. Mystical religion, because of its individualism and anarchism, tends to the rejection of the traditional Church-type of Christianity. It reacts against the institutionalism and authoritarian conformism of the religious establishment. For that reason there is an affinity between mystical Christianity and the modern insistence upon freedom and subjectivity. The question, however, is whether the acknowledgment of the freedom of the individual subject as a fundamental value, both spiritually and politically, necessarily implies the reduction of the Church to a scattering of purely voluntary associations, the impermanent products of a variety of individual initiatives. How can we conceive of the Church as a social reality superordinate to the individual, a spiritual power higher than any product of free collaboration, and do so without reverting to the heteronomy of the traditional conception of the Church? Freedom is a fundamental value, because it is the condition of possibility for the emergence of other values, both individual and social, but the Church is a community created by God's grace and is in that sense prior to the exercise of human freedom. My suggestion, which has some historical support, is that we forge a new conception of the Church by bringing together the insights embodied in the formation of the bourgeois public sphere and the experience of the Church as a mystical or transcendent community. Mystical religion will thus be given political value as a principle or ground for an ongoing critique of institutional religion.

The temptation, however, of the theologian, always threatened by philosophic idealism, is to suppose that a public exists because we talk about it. David Tracy has fallen into that temptation in *The Analogical*

Imagination.[104] In that book, he insists upon the essential publicness of theology. In developing this theme, he distinguishes three publics of theology: society, the academy, and the Church. Surprisingly enough, although he makes frequent reference to Habermas on other points, he does not refer to Habermas's account of the bourgeois public. For Tracy a public is simply without further analysis a reference group, an addressee of theology. All theology is addressed to all three reference groups or publics, but there is a special relationship between each of the three branches of theology and a particular public. Fundamental theology is primarily directed to the academy and is concerned primarily to provide arguments that all reasonable persons, whether religiously involved or not, can recognize as reasonable. Systematic theology is addressed primarily to the Church, understood as a community of moral and religious discourse and action. The major concern is the reinterpretation of the particular tradition to which the theologian belongs. Practical theology is addressed primarily to society. It is related to some social, political, cultural, or pastoral concerns taken as possessing major religious import.

Tracy's failure, however, to examine the concrete, historical reality of the three publics leaves his analysis the expression of a vague aspiration rather than a description of theology as it actually exists.

Take what he terms the public of the Church. Tracy is a Catholic theologian. Is the Catholic Church a public in the sense of a community of discourse, exercising a surveillance and critique over the teaching and action of those holding authority within it? It is not. There are groups within that Church wanting the Church to become a public in that sense, but the present institutional setup for the Church embodies a claim to moral sovereignty, namely, a claim that there is in the Church a center of ultimate reference, having the last word and demanding obedience to whatever it decrees or declares. To advocate a critical public is precisely to deny the existence of such moral sovereignty.

As for society, we have already seen that the development of monopoly capitalism and its exploitation of the mass media have prevented the formation of a critical public and turned public opinion from being a rational product into a manipulated result. What audience exists in society today for serious theology? Tracy acknowledges the marginalization of theology and of humanistic reflection generally in our society, dominated as it is by the instrumental rationality of technology, but he does not seem to regard this as affecting the very conditions of possibility of theology. Is theology possible in a society without a critical public, where discourse is prevented?

Finally, one may likewise question whether the academy constitutes a public for the rational discourse of fundamental theology. It is fragmented into specialties closed off from one another, and within it humanistic reflection is almost as marginalized as in the wider society.

In brief, is not the addressee of theological work such as Tracy's simply other theologians? This means that it does not possess the publicness Tracy himself considers essential to it.

To discuss how far it is possible to create anything corresponding to the bourgeois critical public in society or the academy today exceeds the scope of these reflections. But we may ask how the Churches could by their own example point the way to the social embodiment of freedom in a community of discourse.

Let us return to the theme of the emergence of a new conception of the Church in the nineteenth century. Alexander Dru names Johann Michael Sailer (1751–1823) as the one chiefly responsible for the new development. He quotes Geiselmann to the effect that

> it is not to Möhler, or even to Scheeben, but to Johann Michael Sailer that we owe the fact that the theology of the nineteenth century rediscovered the mystical conception of the Church as opposed to the legal conception derived from the controversial theology (of the post-reformation period).[105]

In an essay on Sailer, Geiselmann sees the development of his concept of the Church as falling into three periods.[106] In the first period he was still dominated by the influence of his teacher, Benedict Stattler (1728–1797), for whom in accordance with post-Tridentine ecclesiology generally the Church was viewed simply in social and legal terms, so that it was conceived of as a supernatural, visible society, hierarchical in structure and endowed with rights. The influence of the *Aufklärung* had penetrated this concept to the extent that the Church was seen primarily as an ethical institution. In the second period Sailer had come under the influence of the mystical tradition, which he encountered through Lavater, Matthias Claudius, and the Pietists. It was through them he became acquainted with Suso, Tauler, Eckhart, Fénelon, whom Claudius translated, Teresa of Avila, and John of the Cross.[107] His concept of the Church during this period was that of a living mediator of a living piety. One lived from the Church and in the Church. As yet, however, one was not seen as living the Church. It was under the influence of the Romantic conception of community that Sailer moved in the third period to the concept of the Church as the living form, the public embodiment of a common spiritual life and tradition. Here, then, is the full concept of the Church as the mystical Body of Christ, which Sailer sees as ideally but not factually coincident with the visible Church.[108]

What all that means is that the inadequacy of the *Aufklärung* conception of the Church from a Christian standpoint was met by drawing upon the mystical tradition and expanding its contribution under the impact of the Romantic movement.

A similar confluence of modernity and mysticism is found in Protestant theology. According to Troeltsch, while modernity provoked the decay of the pure Church-type as a Christian social form, the Church-type has persisted in a modified version under the influence of mysticism and idealism.[109] He sees in Schleiermacher the emergence of a new concept of Church which transcends the distinction between the Church-type and the sect-type. This regards the Church as a religious community involving the active participation of the individual and yet as having a generative power superordinate to the individual, an organic radiation from a nodal point. This conceives the Church according to the organic notion of the nature of community, stressed in the Romantic movement.[110]

The promise of the early nineteenth century was not fulfilled. The impact of the restoration movement upon theology blocked the development of the new concept of the Church and brought a return to the heteronomous and hierarchical concept of Church authority. Insofar as the new concept remained current, it did so as a theological fantasy, an ideal ungrounded in the actual reality of the Church. The problem of the Church is not primarily an intellectual one but a matter of the restructuring of the Church on the basis of the principle of freedom. The nineteenth century reconceived the Church, but did not succeed in creating a new sociological form in the concrete. That problem still remains with us, though now in altered conditions.

The suggestion I have been making is that mystical religion need not be a principle of social withdrawal or of anarchism but could become the spiritual form of the principle of freedom for a reconstruction of the Church. That mysticism can have such a socially critical function is illustrated, for example, in the life and writings of Thomas Merton. If called upon in that way, mystical religion can make a contribution that will prevent a pragmatic version of Christian faith from becoming a mere humanism or worldly activism.

CHAPTER 11

Conclusion: What Is Left of Christianity?

The presupposition of the analysis of various forms of Christian religion I have just completed is that Christianity may be understood as a symbol system or, better, as a set of differently organized symbol systems, all drawing upon a common stock of symbols. Now there are those for whom any such interpretation means the destruction of Christianity, because it removes the scandal of particularity and of consequent exclusivity, which is of the very essence of Christian faith, constituting its distinctive truth. That objection has indeed much force and demands to be treated with the greatest respect. Let me, then, first elaborate it as well as I can.

Christian belief, so it is argued, is not content to declare that humanity manifests the divine; it affirms that God became this particular man, Jesus of Nazareth, born at a particular time and place. To be a Christian it is not enough to find meaningful the imagery of a dying and rising god; one is asked to declare one's belief that this man, Jesus of Nazareth, who is the incarnate Son of God, suffered under the Roman procurator Pontius Pilate for the sins of his fellow men and women, was crucified, died, and was buried and on the third day at a particular point in time rose again for their justification. At the center of the Christian creed there is not the myth of a dying and rising god, an archetypal image of a general truth about humanity and its relationship to cosmic reality, but a single and singular historical and cosmic event.

This anchoring of abstract, generalized imagery in concrete particular persons and events pervades the entire Christian mentality. At Christmas Christians do not celebrate childhood, but the birth of a particular baby. Mary is not the Eternal Feminine or the Great Mother but a real, individual woman. The disciples were not personified responses or attributes but a group of actual men, each with his own individualized history. The Church is not an intangible, idealized community, but an identifiable social entity, imperfect as human but preserving essentially intact down through the centuries the revealed truth given by God through Jesus and the memory of the events in which it was given.

That account of Christianity does not deny a correspondence, or even coincidence, between the expression of Christian truths and the archetypal images and age-old symbolism of myths as found universally. In making his final revelation, God could be expected to take up, correct, and fulfill the symbolic heritage of humankind's religious history, a symbolism rooted in the structures of the human psyche. But Christian belief is that in the events, actions, and words of Jesus Christians passed from a state of pagan ignorance to a knowledge of the living God and of God's plan in Jesus Christ for the salvation of humankind.

Pagan religion is indeed an affair of images, symbols, myths, arising from the unconscious; it is irrational or, at least, prerational. With Christian revelation, so the objection continues, we move from pagan darkness into the clear light of history and reason. We can hardly speak of beliefs or doctrines in relation to the pagan religions, because they had no firm teaching but were the imaginative expression of yearning and desire. For that reason Christianity with its doctrinal affirmations has more affinity with pagan philosophy than with pagan religion. From its beginning Christianity was conscious of being able to formulate and affirm the truth concerning God, humankind, the universe, and history. It was not left wandering in the shadowland of imaginative stories, mythical dreams, and the magical manipulation of unknown forces.

Admittedly, most objectors to my analysis would today concede that the other major world religions, notably, Hinduism, Buddhism, and Islam, cannot be dismissed as examples of pagan ignorance but do mediate important religious insights and truths. All the same, the scandal of particularity, namely, the once-for-all character of Christian revelation, requires Christians to see in Jesus of Nazareth a unique historical and cosmic event embodying the definitive action and revelation of God for human salvation. This necessarily implies that other religions purvey only partial truth, calling for correction and completion by the fullness of Christian revelation.

In sum, the objection to my identification of Christian religion with a range of symbol systems is that I have thrust Christian faith back into the irrational. I have reduced Christian teaching to the symbolic sources and imaginative elements it draws upon, and in doing so I have lost its distinctive affirmation of historical fact and supernaturally revealed truth. Although, for example, Christian teaching draws upon a changing variety of symbols to express the meaning of the crucifixion, it steadfastly affirms it as a unique event embodying the definitive action of God for human salvation. Christian teaching is not just a series of images, myths, and symbols collected for meditative use, but a set of affirmations concerning what is in reality the case with our relationship to God, the world, history, and our fellow human beings. What is left after my account is not Christianity at all. I have failed to distinguish revealed truth from myth.

The view of Christianity on which the objection is based has a powerful appeal. Provided a person can avoid coming to grief on some of the more difficult doctrines, he or she is offered the immense assurance of clearly knowing the fundamental truths concerning human origin, life, and destiny. One might well see that assurance as underlying the confidence of the West in the superiority of its own civilization, which it felt right to export to the furthest reaches of the globe. Why, then, has this conception of Christian revelation lost its hold upon people's minds? I do not say lost its appeal, because many would like to be able still to affirm it but are unable to retain their former conviction. There has been a widespread collapse of the ability to affirm what is regarded as the literal truth of Christianity, while at the same time people cling to the Christian religion as an expression of their yearning, their hope, and indeed their belief in a deeper reality, a better world, a higher existence than that of their everyday experience. Does this mark the twilight of Christian faith, or is it, instead, a shift to a sounder interpretation of religious language?

The basic flaw in what I may call the "literalist" or "realist" account of Christianity is that it attempts to combine the certitude of myth with the rationality of intellectual discourse. It wants to make the transition from *mythos* to *logos* without surrendering the warm certitudes of myth.

To move from myth to reason in the sense of *logos* is, with explicit reflection, to limit what one affirms as certain or even only as probable to what is supported by reasons sufficient to sustain what is affirmed. To affirm a factual state of affairs thus requires that the content of the affirmation be verified in the relevant data. The precise control of the knowing process by rational criteria brings with it the recognition that human knowledge is limited, indeed fragmentary, for the most part only approximating to the truth, and consequently, even if we ignore for the moment the occurrence of error, subject to continual revisions. When reason is in control, we can affirm individual items of knowledge as certain; but as soon as we attempt to develop explanatory theories or wide-ranging syntheses, we are dealing with the hypothetical and the probable and must be prepared for the constant replacement of one theory or synthesis by another.

It is not to my purpose here to give an analysis of the process of scientific knowledge, nor do I wish to maintain that verification and argumentation in all branches of knowledge follow the same procedures and criteria as in the natural sciences. My limited aim is to underline the contention that if one takes one's stand upon reason, there is no way in which one can affirm the set of propositions constituting the body of Christian doctrine—or any other set of religious doctrines for that matter—as verified, factual, unchanging certainties.

At this point it is usual to make appeal to divine revelation. Reason, it is said, may not be able directly to establish those doctrines; indeed, rational proof is excluded because they are supernatural truth. But reason can provide sufficient grounds for affirming that they are divinely revealed.

Any such appeal merely pushes the difficulty back a stage. There is no way in which reason can discriminate among the various claimants to divine revelation or determine precisely the content of any particular claimant with sufficient cogency to justify affirming a set of doctrinal propositions as divinely revealed certainties.

The very attempt to combine reasons as controlling the process of knowledge and revelation as a body of authoritative doctrines is a cultural hybrid. It produces an unstable amalgam of elements from two different and incompatible cultural ideals. The appeal to revelation belongs to a culture in which the important truths concerning human life and society are handed down in a tradition by teachers having authority and are proclaimed for acceptance as sacred. The appeal to reason, on the contrary, presupposes an open community of discourse in which all the members participate in seeking knowledge and in which any claim to acceptance must rest upon evidence and argumentation open to scrutiny and criticism by all. Scientists have achieved such a community, but within a limited field. It became, however, a wider cultural ideal from at least the Enlightenment.

Now one might well contend that reason in its logical and critical function is an inadequate guide to human life because it cannot provide more than a variety of hypotheses and some probable conclusions. It can serve only as a subordinate tool. Tradition, on the other hand, does embody a cumulative wisdom; it provides the practical certitude that comes from living out over generations the insights and values of a way of life. But this is in effect to argue for the permanence of myth, which is the symbolic expression of the traditional insights and values of a society. What is inconsistent is to claim for a set of propositional doctrines the unhesitating and unquestioning certitude that belongs to myth in its practical function. Once one has left myth and entered into conceptual analysis and carefully measured rational affirmations, one is confined to the limited, tentative results of theoretical reflection, results always subject to further development, reformulation, and revision. What I have called the literalist interpretation of Christianity is an attempt to claim the certitude proper to myth for a rationally constructed set of factual assertions. Such certitude is simply not, in principle, available.

The clearest illustration of the inconsistency I have been pointing out is the checkered theological career of historical criticism of the Bible.[111] Once one accepts that the Bible like any other book or set of documents is subject to the canons of historical criticism, then one must renounce the certainty claimed by the literalist interpretation for the factual assertions of biblical history. On the basis of such documents as are found in the Bible, historians cannot claim more than probability for their individual assertions nor regard any wide-ranging reconstructions as more than tentative hypotheses.

Thus, in the first place, historical criticism has played havoc with the traditional attributions of date and authorship, to which appeal was made when asserting the authority of the biblical books. No longer can the theologian point to the Mosaic authorship of the Pentateuch, the Davidic authorship of the Psalms, the Isaian authorship of the Servant Songs, the Pauline authorship of the Pastoral Epistles, and so on, to support the divine origin and authority of the content of those sacred books. What has resulted is not the mere replacement of the traditional authors with their disciples or less prestigious writers but the uncovering of the immersion of the biblical texts in the myriad contingencies of history. The typical biblical book does not come down to us all of a piece from some acknowledged prophetic figure or divine messenger but as the documentary sediment of the history of a people, with originating factors too complex for disentanglement with more than changing probability. This has changed our understanding of the authority of a biblical text. It is not that of an oracle from on high but that of an expression of the religious identity of a particular people.

That identity, though historical, cannot derive its normativeness from historical criticism, because it is constituted by the free, undetermined response of the people to the changing events and circumstances of its history. Recently, in his excellent *The Uses of Scripture in Recent Theology*;[112] David Kelsey has convincingly argued that when a theologian says, "Scripture is authoritative for theology," he is not putting forward a descriptive claim about the biblical texts and their special properties. He is not, in other words, expressing an historical or literary judgment on those texts. He is making a policy decision. He is committing himself to using those texts in a normative fashion. His declaration is a self-involving, performative utterance. He is setting up the rule he commits himself to follow when he does theology.

"Scripture is authoritative for theology" is part of the meaning of the wider, "Scripture is authoritative for the life of the Church," which itself is the same as saying, "These biblical texts are Scripture." Again, this does not make a descriptive claim, assigning some peculiar property to the texts, which can be verified independently of a commitment or policy decision. It is to say that these texts must be used in certain ways in the common life of the Church. One of the activities in the common life of the Church for which the biblical texts are used is doing theology. To say that Scripture is authoritative for the Church is to acknowledge that the use of the biblical texts is essential to establishing and preserving the identity of the Christian community. The Church in declaring the biblical writings as Christian Scripture is acknowledging its own continuing self-identity. Insofar as "doing theology" is understood as a activity within the common life of the Church, namely, as the activity by which the Church self-consciously criticizes her own faithfulness to her task, then "Scripture is authoritative for theology" is analytic in "Scripture is authoritative for the Church." Its authority for theology does not rest upon particular historical or literary judgments about the biblical texts.

A similar interpretation of the authority of Church doctrines has been put forward recently by George Lindbeck in his *The Nature of Doctrine: Religion and Theology in a Postliberal Age.*[113] He has been struck, as others have been, by the strange outcome of ecumenical dialogue in which doctrines once really opposed are now really reconcilable, even though the two positions remain identical to what they were before. Thus Anglicans and Catholics find their positions on the Eucharist are really reconcilable, even though neither side feels that they have surrendered their traditional teaching. So there is now agreement where in the past martyrs have died for the difference. Reflecting upon this ecumenical experience, Lindbeck has concluded that doctrines, when they are functioning as communal doctrines, namely, as norms of communal belief and action, are second-order, not first-order, statements. First-order statements directly refer to religious realities and make truth-claims about them. Second-order statements are statements about statements; they formulate rules of discourse. He argues, then, that doctrines when functioning as dogmas or communal norms, do not make first-order truth-claims. They function as rules for the discourse of the community, excluding some truth-claims and permitting others. They do not specify positively what is to be affirmed but remain open to a permissible plurality of beliefs. Doctrinal propositions may indeed be taken up by the devout or by theologians and developed as first-order propositions, but when so used they are not functioning as Church doctrines. Doctrines have their authority not by their content, which is illustrative rather than determinative, but as community rules, preserving the identity of the community in a particular historical situation and within the cultural linguistic system it has elaborated for its life.

To return now to the authority of Scripture for theology and the Church. It is not merely that the general religious authority of the biblical texts cannot be established by historical criticism but also that no particular historical interpretation of their content can impose itself with the certitude required by the literalist account of Christian doctrines.

Take the central issue, namely, the interpretation of the data concerning Jesus Christ. Historians differ about whether Jesus made any personal messianic claims. The differing conclusions are not entirely attributable to different presuppositions on the part of the historians. The patent fact is that the data are insufficient to ground an historical certainty in this matter. Hence we have to be content with a number of equally probable conclusions. There will always be a variety of historical lives of Jesus, not only because historians work with different fundamental presuppositions, but also because the data are scanty and leave the way wide open to a variety of probable reconstructions. In addition to that, the New Testament itself contains a variety of Christologies, that is, of interpretations of the life and work of Jesus. That is not indeed surprising, once one recognizes that Christology is the symbolic elaboration of the religious meaning made manifest in Jesus, because symbols are not mutually exclusive in the same way as factual assertions or logically formulated propositions.

There is a contrast here between two fundamentally different ways of talking about the Incarnation: the symbolic and the ontological.

Symbolic talk about the Incarnation has its source and ground in a shared experience of the person of Jesus of Nazareth as the bearer of mystery. I say "shared" because the experience of the presence of mystery in Jesus is not an asocial, ahistorical, individualist affair, but an experience which comes to the individual through belonging to a tradition, joining in a common worship, and taking part in the life of a community of disciples. All the same, though it comes only through a process of mediation, there is for each Christian an experience of Jesus Christ as the manifestation of mystery. "Mystery" here refers to the term or goal of the human orientation towards ultimate reality, power, and meaning, towards transcendent freedom, absolute hope, and unconditional love. The use of the word "mystery" indicates that this goal or term of the movement of the human spirit is beyond the limits of human knowledge, beyond description or direct conception. Consequently it can be expressed only indirectly through a variety of symbols and metaphors. Through the story of Jesus of Nazareth, through the tradition of his words and deeds, through the sense of his living presence in the communities that are named after him, Christians are led into a way of life embodying meanings and values that find their origin, their justification, and their fulfillment in the unfathomable mystery thus made manifest for them in him. That mystery cannot be directly expressed, nor, consequently, can its relation either to Jesus or to ourselves be described, in cognitively precise terms. The identification of Jesus with God as the Word of God, the Son of God, the glory of God, and so on, states the function of Jesus as mediator and symbolically expresses the presence of mystery in him and through him in ourselves. Furthermore, it is important to note that language concerning Christ, like religious language in general, should not be reduced to the formulation of descriptive statements or assertions of fact, even though some such statements have a limited place. Language about Christ, taken in its full richness, has the rhetorical function of evoking the appropriate experience and of handling the resulting set of relationships with God, Christ, and the Christian community.

In contrast, those who engage in ontological talk about the Incarnation claim that they can make literal statements about the being of Jesus Christ. Lonergan lays out the minimum basis for such ontological talk.[114] The Father, Son, and Spirit are distinct identities. The Son, however, is not a distinct identity with regard to a particular man. The man Jesus of Nazareth did not have his identity in himself but in the eternal Son, so that he was in fact the Son become man. That would seem to be the minimum set of affirmations for any assertion of the Incarnation as literal fact. From there one can proceed to offer a more elaborate account by developing "person" and "nature" as metaphysical concepts (which goes beyond their purely heuristic use by the Council of Chalcedon) and applying such Scholastic metaphysical concepts as *esse*, act, and potency or drawing upon some other metaphysical conceptuality. Let me, however, stay with the minimum, in order to insist upon the question: What would ground the judgment that the man Jesus of Nazareth did not have his identity in himself, but in the second eternal identity of the Trinity, so that he was in fact the Son become man?

That judgment, in the ontological view, makes a factual claim. But it is difficult to see how it could be reached by a process of examining, understanding, and reflecting upon any experiential data. Even the experience of the resurrection of Jesus by his disciples, taken in its strongest form, does not require the factual identity of Jesus with the eternal Son. The assertion that Jesus of Nazareth is God in a literal, ontological sense can be made, it seems to me, only as a believing assent to a revealed proposition or set of propositions with an equivalent meaning. In other words, we have to suppose a propositional revelation, in which already formulated propositions are presented to the believer as of supernatural origin and of divine authority. A set of propositions stating the literal divinity of Jesus is conceived as coming to the believer in the form of a personal claim made by Jesus himself or as the divinely inspired recognition of his true identity by his disciples. The propositions are supported by external signs of their origin.

Two difficulties confront such an account. First, it has no firm historical basis. In the present stage of our historical knowledge, it is improbable that Jesus himself made any claim to divinity in an ontological, literal sense. Furthermore, the disciples did not behave as if they had any already formulated, divinely authorized interpretation of Jesus to rest upon. Somewhat fumblingly and with a variety of results, they struggled to articulate their experience of the person and mission of Jesus with the help of themes, images, and symbols from the Hebrew Bible and the later intertestamental tradition. Secondly, the account supposes a thoroughly mythical conception of divine revelation. That point is worth pursuing further.

The inherent weakness and final unviability of the ontological view of the Incarnation as a mode of interpreting religious language about Jesus Christ is that in its attempts to exclude a mythical conception of the Incarnation it has to fall back upon a mythical conception of divine revelation, in which God is thought of as presenting the mind with a series of already formulated propositional truths. That fundamental inconsistency is another manifestation of the incoherent desire to combine the descriptive precision and conceptual clarity of reason or *logos* with the certitude that belongs to myth but belongs to it, not in any of its symbolic expressions as cognitive representations, but as vehicles of an orientation towards the absolute or transcendent.

To clarify that contention, let me set forth what would be a non-mythical interpretation of divine revelation. This would distinguish faith from beliefs and ground beliefs upon faith.

Faith is the fundamental religious response. It is the orientation towards mystery or unlimited reality accepted or assented to in a self-transcendent response or movement of unrestricted love. This faith-love is divine revelation in the primary sense of the presence of the divine reality in our minds and hearts. As responded to, it creates a fundamental stance in the subject which, like an originating idea, takes possession of the mind and heart and widens the horizon within which the person thinks, judges, decides, and acts. This gives rise to divine revelation in a secondary sense, namely, a body of religious beliefs, constituting a tradition. The fundamental stance or originating idea provokes and governs the apprehension of values and the formation of judgments of value as these occur in relation to the concrete particularities of historical situations. Judgments of value constitute the first type of religious belief. The second type is judgments of fact. Factual beliefs arise as the mind, animated by faith-love and thus open in an unrestricted fashion to reality, strives to interpret all the date before, both of the external world and of the interior world of consciousness. The struggle to interpret reality, which takes place religiously within the horizon created by the response to utterly transcendent reality, produces insights, formulations of various kinds, and judgments of fact, the latter being factual beliefs.

Both kinds of religious belief—judgments of value and judgments of fact—are thus the product of interpretive reflection by the human mind within the horizon opened up by faith-love. Therefore they are marked by the relativity, mutability, and cultural limitations of all products of human finite intelligence, however illumined. To suppose that religious beliefs, particularly factual beliefs, are ready-made propositions, coming down from on high, stamped as authentic by external signs or miracles, is to take the mythical image of God speaking in a crudely literalist fashion. Divine revelation is the involvement through faith of the divine Spirit in the human, historical process of religious knowledge.

I should add that religious language, as I have already argued in this book, is not exhausted by the articulation of propositional beliefs, whether of judgments of value or of judgments of fact, but has wider rhetorical, poetic, and practical functions.

The certitude, then, which we regard as characteristic of religious beliefs does not accrue to them as descriptive, factual statements or as evaluative judgments. In that function they are relative, changeable, and more often probable rather than certain. Their basic certitude is as vehicles of the faith-experience of mystery. This certitude tends to spill over into religious language in its other functions, because these serve to mediate the faith-experience in a detailed way into every area of thought, feeling, and action. The question is whether we should limit "truth" to the correctness of propositional statements or see "truth" more deeply as a quality of human subjects as they struggle for authenticity in dealing, intellectually, imaginatively, and practically with reality? Such questing authenticity does not demand the permanence, unrevisability, or certitude of any particular religious item or result—any more than to be a true scientist requires an unchallengable certainty of scientific statements.

In sum, ontological talk about the Incarnation forgets the limitations of human thought and language. The doctrines of the Trinity and of the Incarnation are symbolic constructs. They have an objective reference, insofar as they mediate the relationship of the subject to the reality of mystery. But the term of the relationship remains unknown as mystery, beyond the ability of the subject to do more than affirm its presence, assent to its transforming influence, and articulate its meaning in a variable series of images, symbols, and metaphors. The symbolic content of the two doctrines has a prehistory, and the doctrines themselves emerged gradually in the Christian tradition. They thus bear the marks of the creativity of the human religious imagination. The attempt to turn their imaginative content into ontological statements is as misguided as the turning of the religious account of creation into a statement of geological fact.

There is a misunderstanding here of the nature and function of Christian realism. In general, Christian realism gives a name to the conviction that Christianity, unlike other religions, does not allow the untrammeled exuberance of the religious imagination its head but checks it, so that the Christian religion has to come to grips with the actual reality of human life and destiny in the setting of society and the cosmos as they actually are. Hence, sobriety is a characteristic of Christian symbolism, in contrast to the weird and wonderful creations of the unchecked religious imagination elsewhere.

A valid point is being made there, as anyone will admit who compares the Bible to any collection of myths, even though we must allow for the way familiarity dulls our perception of biblical imaginative excesses. But it is a mistake to attach Christian realism to the process of doctrinalization and to identify it with an epistemological realism that translates symbolic statements into ontological assertions. Christian realism is more properly associated with the predominance in the Bible of realistic narrative as a literary form and with the everyday content of the parables as the chief teaching medium in the New Testament.

I have already, following Frei,[115] explained that realistic narrative, as understood in this context, predates the distinction between history and fiction. Realistic narrative in the biblical sense is not history in the modern sense, namely, an empirically accurate report of events as they actually occurred. The empirical and the fictional are indissolubly fused in a complex, undifferentiated form of narrative. That narrative is historylike in its presentation of a common public world, which is the same world as ours, in its depiction of the realization of a theme through the interaction of character and circumstances and in the identity between the story and its meaning. With realistic narrative there is no gap, as there is with allegory and nonrealistic myth, between the representation and what is represented. In other words, the meaning of the narrative is identical with the dynamics of the story.

The prominence of realistic narrative as the chief literary form in Christian religious expression may be linked to what is the greatest difference between the Jewish and Christian traditions of interpretation, which is the dropping of Halakhah altogether by the Christians and the exclusive turning to the New Testament equivalent of Haggadah.[116] (Halakhah and Haggadah were the two components of rabbinic teaching. Halakhah, literally "walking", with reference to Exodus 18:20, "and you shall teach them the statutes and the decisions, and make them know the way in which they must walk and what they must do," was legal teaching. Haggadah, literally "narrative," was nonlegal, devotional teaching.) In the Christian Haggadah the story of Jesus was made central, and all the previous stories from the Jewish Scriptures were lined up in one narrative sequence with the help of a figurative or typological interpretation, in which the allegorical and literal are in some fashion joined. The identity of Jesus and of Christians themselves was thus established by their insertion into a narrative sequence that in its fullness stretched from the creation to the end of the world. And the world in which they were placed and in which they had their identity was the world of ordinary, everyday existence, though constantly the theater of the saving actions of God.

The shaping of Christian Haggadah, including what now became the

Old Testament, into an all-embracing realistic narrative enabled it to serve the function for Christians of the Halakhah, which they had dropped, namely, to relate their religious feelings and beliefs to the actual, concrete reality of their lives, to the nitty-gritty of their day-to-day existence. What the Christian approach emphasized with its use of realistic narrative was that what was important was not any special religious observances or ritual but the transformation of the ordinary actions of their everyday lives. Although this was obscured with the elaborate development of Catholic practices in the Middle Ages, the original Christian insight was that religion did not consist in carrying out specifically religious actions but in the purification, redirection and remotivation of the same human actions as before, now thus transformed by the gift of the Spirit.

The parables of the New Testament fall into line with the same approach. They are stories, this time fictional, in which the incidents and characters are taken from ordinary life. They therefore depict the same world as the one we live in. Again, they are not allegories; their meaning is identical with what happens in the story, a meaning which can be transferred to ourselves. Each parable has a twist which puts its contents under a transcendent perspective, turning ordinariness into extravagance, which is what happens when ordinary lives are transformed by the gift of grace.

To return to the main point: Christian realism is not a stress upon the objective reference of religious propositions; it is not an attitude that focuses upon the capacity of human mind to reach valid knowledge in the realm of religious truth. Christian realism, properly speaking, is the identification of religion with the living out of our ordinary lives in the one world of everyday existence. It is the rejection of a separate sacred world, and an affirmation of the sacredness and meaningfulness of the concrete reality of human, historical life.

Once again we reach the basic principle that what is foundational in Christianity is not knowledge but love. Christianity is a way of life, the result of the transformation of the individual person and the community by the gift of a transcendent love—a love no longer egocentric but self-transcendent in a radical sense and unrestricted, even to the inclusion of enemies; no longer based upon merit or success but persistent in the midst of failure and rejection. As with any attempt to characterize a way of life, such general statements need supplementing by the presentation of various persons as models, exemplifying the embodiment of that way of life in different circumstances. But that goes beyond what I can offer here.

But does not the making of love foundational expose us without protection to every kind of fanaticism? Is not the downgrading of knowledge the very corruption of love, because love must be enlightened and guided by knowledge if it is not to become a destructive force? Surely Christian faith, hope, and love must be grounded in a knowledge of God and of God's saving actions and promises, above all, as manifested in Jesus Christ.

It is remarkable how people are sensitive to the possible corruption of love but not to the frequent distortion of knowledge. Knowledge can be readily twisted into a projection of egocentric interests or neurotic desires and fears; it can so easily become a rationalization of the subject's drive for power, self-protection, or self-aggrandizement. If, as I should agree, objectivity is the other side of authentic subjectivity, then the requisite for genuine, objective knowledge is the purification of the subject, the unrestricted openness of the subject without inhibition or closure to reality. That openness is love in its foundational, unrestricted form as a transcendental orientation.

However, there is a secondary phase in which knowledge is foundational. It is that an immediate task of love in its practical activity must be to acquire the requisite and available knowledge for the work in hand. If one is dealing, for example, with some social problem, then every effort must be made to analyze and understand the problem aright. Far from downgrading knowledge, Christian love can in situations where self-interests, passions, and prejudices are distorting people's assessment lead the way towards an unprejudiced, uninhibited account. Here, too, Christian love properly understood releases into their full functioning rational criteria for the testing and evaluation of proposed solutions or modes of action.

But the human condition is crossed by negativities—notably death, sin, failure, immeasurable and meaningless suffering, which cannot be adequately met, let alone removed, by action within this world. This is the proper sphere of religious faith and its appeal to the truth and power of the Beyond. Here diverse attempts to make knowledge foundational in the form of an authoritative revelation must be judged a failure, because the paradox of religious experience is that, while it converts and convinces the believer, it remains baseless delusion to the unbeliever. What takes possession of the mind and heart of the believer is the reality of love, which is its own justification, even though it finds confirmation in its fruits and in its harmony with the known truths and values available to human intelligence. Religious knowledge, in the form of images, symbols, narratives, doctrines, is the working out of the implications of the experience of the Beyond; it is not the starting-point or foundation.

I have been asking the question, What is left of Christianity? The bearing of my remarks is that it is no longer appropriate, if it ever was, to look to Christianity for an objectively validated account in propositional form of God, the cosmos, human life, and history. We live in a pluralist situation, in which we are becoming increasingly aware of the varying patterns in the experience of the Beyond and varying accounts of the world and the human condition. While there are undoubtedly conflicts and contradictions, there is sufficient convergence for us to look for the complementarity of the major religious traditions and to question claims to an exclusive universality or complete truth.

That is also a reason for developing a suppler analysis of religious language than is found in the literalistic interpretation of Christianity I have been discussing. The inconsistency of that interpretation is that, while proclaiming that Christian truth is not myth, it clings to a mythical approach in refusing to break the myth and acknowledge the symbolic nature of religious expression.

To end on a more positive note, let me change the question, What is left of Christianity? to the question, What is the contribution of Christianity to the present social and cultural situation? I should like to tackle that question by comparing the fears and hesitations of Westerners in regard to Marxism with similar fears and hesitations, less acknowledged, about Christianity. (It is not to my limited purpose here to distinguish the thought of Marx himself from Marxism or to distinguish the various kinds of Marxism.)

Why does the average Westerner, including many strongly critical of the present social order and deeply concerned for social justice, fear a coming to power of Marxism? I am not referring to fears of Soviet world domination, because I am not identifying Soviet Communism with Marxism. Nor have I in mind the pathological anti-Communism that infects some circles—not those concerned with social justice, but those concerned with the maintenance of the status quo. I am referring to a less obvious fear, a fear that prevents people, even those critical of capitalism, from adopting the tolerant attitude of letting the Marxists have a turn to try out their remedies for present ills. It is operative even where, as in Italy, the Marxists have renounced recourse to violent revolution and declared their willingness to submit to the democratic process.

I think the source of that fear is the judgment that, once the Marxists had gained power, they could not within the logic of their system allow any challenge to their rule. They would inevitably repress and eliminate any opposition. Once they were in, there could be no question of future fundamental change or turning back. To allow the Marxists to come to power is to run the risk of closing down the open-ended process of social change and experimentation, which, granted its defects, has been the Western liberal tradition since the Enlightenment.

The instinct of people in this respect is, in my opinion, sound, despite the sincerity of disclaimers by some Marxists and the fact that mere refusal of change or dissent is a capitalist as well as a Marxist characteristic. The fears and hesitations about Marxism rest upon a correct perception of the logic of Marxist doctrine. Marxism puts forward an abstract model of society and history, which it regards as expressing definitive truth. It claims to have unconditional possession of the truth, established once and for all, about society and history. Although Marx proclaimed the primacy of practice over theory, knowledge in the Marxist tradition ceased to be a self-correcting process with fragmentary results, and became an integrated system, based upon the final, unrevisable truth of the historical dialectic. Hence, as people rightly sense, it is difficult to imagine a party convinced that it represents the objective movement of history and that it has the final answers to the problems of human society voluntarily relinquishing its ruling position once it has gained control.

The assurance of the Marxists that they have grasped the truth of how things really are with society and history takes the form of a claim to be scientific. Scientific socialism or Marxism is contrasted with utopian socialism, the latter lacking effective knowledge. Western science, however, has not proceeded on the presuppositions or methods of dialectical materialism and has in general eschewed comprehensive, definitive syntheses as unscientific. To judge from the Soviet despotic system, the claim to unconditional possession of the truth has the most deleterious effects upon the use of reason, once power has been gained. Because it cannot question the order now established, reason is perverted into a legitimizing and rationalizing instrument, serving to justify the system and its actual working. Even within the limited field of Marxist thought itself, Soviet despotism has proved to be utterly stultifying. As Tom Bottomore remarks:

> Dispassionately considered, it is an astonishing phenomenon that in the sixty-five years of existence of the "first workers' state" not a single original work of Marxist social theory has been produced there, and that the further development of Marxist thought has taken place almost entirely in Western Europe.[117]

Now were we to examine that Western development, the so-called critical Marxism, we should reach a less negative assessment of the possible contribution of Marxism to the present social and cultural situation. My point here, however, is the limited one that the appeal of Marxism, even to those who are critical of the present system and eager for radical social change, is blocked by a fear of the freedom-destroying dogmatism inherent in Marxist claims.

However imperfectly they may have been realized in concrete fact, however much they have been abused as a mystification to conceal economic oppression, the ideals of freedom, pluralism, and democracy are rooted deeply in Western culture. These ideals imply, as people recognize, a view of society and history as an open-ended process, a view of human knowledge as incomplete and subject to constant revision, a view of social reform as a matter of trial and error, of debate and experimentation, not as the creation, if necessary through violence, of a perfect society according to a definitive blueprint.

It is my conviction, as I have already made clear, that any fruitful contribution of Christianity to the present situation will presuppose an acceptance of that liberal tradition in its refusal of any dogmatic claim to final, immutable teaching. That is a rejection of dogmatism, whether from the Right or from the Left.

Christian dogmatism in its recent upsurge from the Right is a reactive, sterile formation. It is barren of any creative response to the new challenges of today. Its fundamentalism is the mirror image of the destructive features of modern rationality. This places a one-sided stress upon logic, formal systems, technical language, narrowly conceived empirical verification, and the manipulative, instrumental use of reason, and neglects the imaginative, symbolic, poetic, unformulizable, and communicative functions of reason.

The Christian Left on its part runs the risk of a Marxistlike dogmatism in supposing that there is some radical, clearly delineated, once-for-all solution to the ills of human society. This is not to deny that the critique of Western capitalist society from the Left is in large measure well-founded. But to criticize what is wrong with society is not the same as having a ready-made correct solution to its problems. Again, in many actual situations, Christians are finding in practical action from the Left for social justice the appropriate expression of their Christian faith. But this is not to justify the translation of the absoluteness of Christian love into a political radicalism holding that the present evils of the human condition can be definitively overcome by social and political change and a radically new social order of justice, freedom, and equality created. The negative effect of any such claim is the gap it creates between pretensions and reality, and the attempt to cover over that gap leads inevitably to falsehood, rationalization, and intolerance of criticism.[118]

Meanwhile, a great number of Christians remain unresponsive to the dogmatisms of both Right and Left. Their religious faith is genuine, because they retain a sense of the Beyond. They have a conviction, however unreflective, that human life opens onto a transcendent dimension. But they quietly ignore the continuing dogmatic claims of their official Churches and are even less inclined to go along with the shriller dogmatisms of activists on the Right and Left. The question, however, is how to distinguish their adherence to the liberal tradition of pluralism and tolerance from the torpor of a merely part-commitment. How can a nondogmatic interpretation of Christian faith, such as I have been putting forward in this book, be combined with a tireless living out to the full of the demands of Christian love?

Common action need not have a dogmatic basis, namely, prior agreement on a set of formulated doctrines. As a matter of fact, a dogmatic basis tends to split apart under the pressure of action and cause the formation of disputing factions, as it has done many times in Christian history. Common action may instead be based upon a process of communication. This, if made continuous, can keep creating afresh a common understanding that goes beyond any previously reached agreement, providing thus the flexibility required for action and doing justice to the unity of theory and practice.

What I am calling a process of communication corresponds to the "authentic conversation" of David Tracy, which he distinguishes from "idle chatter, mere debate, gossip or nonnegotiable confrontation."[119] It is likewise the "conversation" Richard Rorty designates as "the ultimate context within which knowledge is to be understood," in contrast to an epistemology-centered philosophy.[120] In relation to the plurality of religions, it is what Wilfred Cantwell Smith calls "colloquy," in order to suggest a side-by-side confronting of humanity's problems rather than a face-to-face confronting of one another.[121] It also coincides with what Habermas analyses as communicative action and rationality in contrast to instrumental action and rationality.[122]

My contention, then, is that the cognitive contribution of Christianity to social, cultural, and political life is to be found in its providing the transcendent foundation needed for sustained communication among human beings, despite their differences and conflicts. The transcendent horizon within which Christian faith places human life, the unrestricted openness to reality it calls for and, though yet imperfectly, creates, the self-transcendence of Christian love, the dignity of each individual resulting from the relation of each person to God, the universal community Christian faith intends and discerns as transcending all social distinctions and indeed the boundary of death itself, so that it includes past victims as well as present liberators: all this provides a basis and context within which human beings can meet together in authentic conversation or colloquy to tackle the problems of human existence through a common understanding and common action, unhindered by fixed, immovable barriers. The Christian Churches, it may be added, are still in possession of an immense organizational network, bringing together at least in an initial fashion people of different social groups and political opinions, which could serve to facilitate authentic conversation or colloquy in our present society, if there was the will to do so.

What, then, is still living in Christianity? Not, I am suggesting, a body of doctrine, containing a formulated worldview and constituting the definitive, literal, and exclusive truth about God, humankind, and the universe. Many practising Christians no longer hold that dogmatic version of their Christian faith, and it seems unlikely to attract many new adherents in the future. More than that, while one can feel some nostalgia for the time when such a view could be held with a calm, innocent assurance, one can only dread, not welcome, any resurgence of such dogmatic literalism in what, after the breaking of the myth, could be only a reactive and destructive form. What is living in Christianity is a way of life, rooted in the experience of the reality of transcendent love and finding its cognitive expression in a symbolic heritage that serves to give continuity to the various patterns of Christian experience, enabling them to pass from the past into the present and from the present into the future.

NOTES

1. Charles Davis, *Theology and Political Society* (Cambridge: Cambridge University Press, 1980), 158–81.
2. Most recently Wilfred Cantwell Smith, *Towards a World Theology: Faith and the Comparative History of Religion* (Philadelphia: Westminster, 1981).
3. I have in mind in particular Rosemary Ruether, *Faith and Fratricide: The Theological Roots of Anti-Semitism* (New York: Seabury Press, 1974).
4. Terry Eagleton, *Walter Benjamin; or Towards a Revolutionary Criticism* (London: Verso, 1981), 98.
5. Ibid., 98.
6. Robert N. Bellah, *Beyond Belief* (New York: Harper & Row, 1970), 21.
7. I am here reproducing some paragraphs from my essay "The Experience of God and the Search for Images," in Axel Steuer and James McClendon, eds., *Is God GOD?* (Nashville: Abingdon, 1982), 37–53.
8. Ian I. Ramsey, *Religious Language: An Empirical Placing of Theological Phrases* (New York: Macmillan, Macmillan Paperbacks Edition, 1963).
9. See *Body As Spirit: The Nature of Religious Feeling* (New York: Seabury Press, 1976), especially chapter 1.
10. Cf. I. A. Richards, *The Philosophy of Rhetoric* (New York: Oxford University Press, 1965), 116–7.
11. Paul Ricoeur, "Biblical Hermeneutics," *Semeia* 4(1975): 107–128.
12. Op.cit., 55–102.
13. Timothy J. Reiss, *The Discourse of Modernism* (Ithaca and London: Cornell University Press, 1982).
14. See Michel Foucault, *Les mots et les choses: Une archéologie des sciences humaines* (Paris: Gallimard, 1966).
15. Hayden White, *Metahistory: The Historical Imagination in Nineteenth-Century Europe* (Baltimore and London: Johns Hopkins University Press, 1973); Hayden White, *Tropics of Discourse: Essays in Cultural Criticism* (Baltimore and London: Johns Hopkins University Press, 1978).
16. Kenneth Burke, *A Grammar of Motives* (Berkeley and Los Angeles: University of California Press, 1969), 503–17.
17. See Hayden White, *Tropics of Discourse,* chapter 9: "The Tropics of History: The Deep Structure of the *New Science,*" 197–217.
18. Roman Jakobson, "The Cardinal Dichotomy in Language," in Ruth Nanda Anshen, ed., *Language: An Enquiry into its Meaning and Function* (New York: Harper, 1957), 155–73. For a brief account of Jakobson's theories, see Terence Hawkes, *Structuralism and Semiotics* (London: Methuen, 1977), 76–87. For a discussion of metaphor and metonymy in the light of Jakobson's analysis, including a footnote explaining why the author prefers Jakobson's account to that of Hayden White, see David Lodge, *The Modes of Modern Writing: Metaphor, Metonymy, and the Typology of Modern Literature* (London: Edward Arnold, 1977), 73–124.
19. Northrop Frye, *Anatomy of Criticism: Four Essays* (New York: Atheneum, 1968), 158–239.
20. Stephen C. Pepper, *World Hypotheses: A Study in Evidence* (Berkeley and Los Angeles: University of California Press, 1957).

21. Karl Mannheim, *Ideology and Utopia: An Introduction to the Sociology of Knowledge* (Harcourt, Brace & World, Harvest Books, 1936).
22. Hayden White, *Metahistory*, 9.
23. Christopher Dawson, *Progress and Religion: An Historical Enquiry* (London: Sheed & Ward, Unicorn Books, 1938), 161–62.
24. Ibid., 258.
25. Dom Columba Marmion, *Christ in His Mysteries* (London: Sands; St Louis: Herder, 1924).
26. Brian A. Gerrish, *Tradition and the Modern World: Reformed Theology in the Nineteenth Century* (Chicago and London: University of Chicago Press, 1978).
27. Op.cit., xi.
28. See Richard Rorty, *Philosophy and the Mirror of Nature* (Princeton: Princeton University Press, 1979), chapter 1: "The Invention of the Mind."
29. Albert William Levi, *Philosophy As Social Expression* (Chicago and London: University of Chicago Press), 199. Levi's italics.
30. Timothy J. Reiss, *The Discourse of Modernism* (Ithaca and London: Cornell University Press, 1982), 30. Reiss's italics.
31. Ibid., 31.
32. Ibid., 49.
33. See Adolf Harnack's account in his *What is Christianity?* (New York: Harper, Harper Torchbook Edition, 1957).
34. Hans Frei, *The Eclipse of Biblical Narrative: A Study in Eighteenth and Nineteenth Century Hermeneutics* (New Haven and London: Yale University Press, 1974).
35. Hans Frei, op.cit., 16.
36. Trutz Rendtorff, *Christentum ausserhalb der Kirche: Konkretion der Aufklärung* (Hamburg: Furche, 1969).
37. Jürgen Habermas, *Strukturwandel der Öffentlichkeit: Untersuchungen zu einer Kategorie der bürgerlichen Gesellschaft* (Neuwied: Luchterhand, 1962).
38. As quoted in Lee H. Yearley, *The Ideas of Newman; Christianity and Human Religiosity* (University Park and London: Pennsylvania State University Press, 1978), 93.
39. Yearley, op.cit., 94.
40. H. A. Enno Van Gelder, *The Two Reformations in the* 16th Century: A Study of the Religious Aspects and Consequences of Renaissance and Humanism (The Hague: Nijhoff, 1964).
41. H. R. Trevor-Roper, *Religion, the Reformation and Social Change and Other Essays* (London: Macmillan, 1967), 219–20.
42. Friedrich Heer, *Die Dritte Kraft: Der europäische Humanismus zwischen den Fronten des konfessionellen Zeitalters.* (Frankfurt am Main: Fischer, 1960.
43. George Tyrrell, *Christianity at the Cross-Roads* (London: Allen & Unwin, 1963; First edition 1909).
44. Op.cit., 21–2.
45. For convenience I have used the text as reprinted in John Hick, ed., *The Existence of God* (New York: Macmillan, 1964).
46. Op.cit., 245.
47. See Alvin W. Gouldner, *The Two Marxisms: Contradictions and Anomalies in the Development of Theory* (New York: Seabury, Continuum Books 1980).
48. Ernst Troeltsch, *The Social Teaching of the Christian Churches* (London: Allen & Unwin, 1931), 2: 734.
49. Ibid., 2: 994.
50. Cf. Leszek Kolakowski, *Chrétiens sans Eglise: La Conscience religieuse et le lien confessionnel au XVII siècle.* Bibliothèque de Philosophie NRF (Paris: Gallimard, 1969), 389–405.
51. Michael Goulder, ed., *Incarnation and Myth: The Debate Continued* (Grand Rapids: Eerdmans, 1979), 10.
52. Karl Rahner *Foundations of Christian Faith: An Introduction to the Idea of Christianity* (London: Darton, Longman & Todd, 1978), 314.

53. See Bernard Lonergan, *Method in Theology* (London: Darton, Longman & Todd, 1972), 85–96.
54. Cf. Peter Berger in Peter Berger, ed., *The Other Side of God: A Polarity in World Religions* (Garden City, New York: Doubleday, Anchor Books 1981), 13.
55. For the relation of the sciences to metaphysics in the synthesis of Aristotle, see Bernard Lonergan, *Verbum: Word and Idea in Aquinas* (London: Darton, Longman & Todd, 1968), vii–viii.
56. See Richard Rorty, *Philosophy and the Mirror of Nature* (Princeton: Princeton University Press, 1979), especially 131–64.
57. Bernard Lonergan, *Insight: A Study of Human Understanding,* revised students' edition (London: Longmans, 1958).
58. Charles Davis, "Lonergan and the Teaching Church," in Philip McShane, *Foundations of Theology: Papers from the International Lonergan Congress* 1970 (Dublin: Gill and Macmillan, 1971), 60–75.
59. I argue the point on the basis of Lonergan's earlier writings in the essay cited in the preceding footnote. Although I think the conclusion still stands, to be fully convincing it would now have to be re-argued in the light of the much more flexible approach of his later writings.
60. *Insight,* 121–28.
61. *Insight,* 118.
62. *Insight,* 125–26.
63. In *A Second Collection: Papers by Bernard J. F. Lonergan,* ed. William F. J. Ryan and Bernard J. Tyrrell (London: Darton, Longman & Todd, 1974), 239–61.
64. Ibid., 261.
65. *Insight,* 697.
66. See his account of praxis in his article, "The Ongoing Genesis of Methods," *SR: Studies in Religion/Sciences Religieuses* 6, no. 4 (1976–7): 351–52; for my critique, see "Lonergan's Appropriation of the Concept of *Praxis,*" *New Blackfriars* 62 (March 1981): 114–26.
67. "The Future of Christianity," in *A Second Collection: Papers by Bernard J.R. Lonergan,* 159.
68. *Method in Theology,* 118.
69. The literature is already extensive. For a first orientation, see Christopher Norris, *Deconstruction: Theory and Practice* (London and New York: Methuen, 1982), and Vincent B. Leitch, *Deconstructive Criticism: Advanced Introduction* (New York: Columbia University Press, 1983).
70. See *Deconstruction and Theology* (New York: Crossroad, 1982), Mark C. Taylor, *Deconstructing Theology* (New York: Crossroad; Chico, Calif.: Scholars Press, 1982), Mark C. Taylor, *Erring: A Postmodern A/theology* (Chicago and London: University of Chicago Press, 1984), and Louis Mackey, "Slouching Toward Bethlehem: Deconstructive Strategies in Theology," *Anglican Theological Review* 65 (1983): 255–72.
71. See Robert Detweiler, ed., *Derrida and Biblical Studies. Semeia* 23 (Chico, Calif.: Scholars Press, 1982).
72. Jacques Derrida, *Writing and Difference* (Chicago: University of Chicago Press, 1978), 292.
73. Fergus Kerr, "Derrida's Wake," *New Blackfriars* 55 (1974): 460.
74. Fergus Kerr, op.cit., 460.
75. The two essays have been brought together in John Stuart Mill, *On Bentham and Coleridge,* introduction by F. R. Leavis (New York: Harper, Harper Torchbooks: The Academy Library, 1962). Here I am reproducing with some changes a paper given to the Nineteenth Century Theology Working Group of the American Academy of Religion and previously printed in Garrett Green and Marilyn C. Massey, eds., *Papers of the Nineteenth Century Theology Working Group: AAR 1982 Annual Meeting* (Berkeley, California; Graduate Theological Union, 1982.
76. Mill, op.cit., 95.
77. Mill, op.cit., 59.

78. Mill, op.cit., 95.
79. *The Novels of Thomas Love Peacock,* edited with introductions and notes by David Garnett (London: Rupert Hart-Davis, 1948), 381.
80. The full phrase is "fluent Benthamites and muddled Coleridgians." I take it from a footnote in G.M. Young, *Victorian England: Portrait of An Age,* 2d. ed. (London, New York and Toronto: Geoffrey Cumberlege, Oxford University Press, 1953), 68, n.2, where we read: "One critic divided the rising generation into fluent Benthamites and muddled Coleridgians."
81. John Coulson, *Newman and the Common Tradition: A Study in the Language of Church and Society* (Oxford: Clarendon Press, 1970), 4. Coulson's italics.
82. Stephen Prickett, *Romanticism and Religion: The Tradition of Coleridge and Wordsworth in the Victorian Church* (Cambridge: Cambridge University Press, 1976), 11. Prickett's italics.
83. Mill, op.cit., 58.
84. Mill, op.cit., 70.
85. Young, *Victorian England,* 68, n.2.
86. For a superb account of the shift from classical to modern ethical theory, see Alasdair MacIntyre, *After Virtue: A Study in Moral Theory* (Notre Dame, Indiana: University of Notre Dame Press, 1981).
87. See Jürgen Habermas, *Strukturwandel der Öffentlichkeit.*
88. John Coulson, *Newman and the Common Tradition,* 50.
89. *The Comedy of Dante Alighieri the Florentine: Cantica I Hell (L'Inferno),* Dorothy L. Sayers, trans. (Harmondsworth: Penguin, Penguin Classics, 1960), 95.
90. John Dominic Crossan, *The Dark Interval: Towards a Theology of Story* (Niles, Illinois: Argus Communications, 1975).
91. M.H. Abrams, *Natural Supernaturalism: Tradition and Revolution in Romantic Literature* (New York: Norton, Norton Library, 1973).
92. Op.cit., 65.
93. Op.cit., 62–63.
94. Op.cit., 334.
95. For a more detailed discussion of our experience of God, see Charles Davis, *Body As Spirit: The Nature of Religious Feeling* (London: Hodder & Stoughton; New York: Seabury, 1976), 17–34, and Charles Davis, "The Experience of God and the Search for Images," in Axel Steuer and James McClendon, eds., *Is God GOD?* (Nashville: Abingdon, 1982), 37–53.
96. For recent statements, see Steven T. Katz, "Language, Epistemology, and Mysticism," in Steven T. Katz, *Mysticism and Philosophical Analysis* (London: Sheldon Press, 1978), 22–74; James R. Horne, "Pure Mysticism and Twofold Typologies: The Typology of Mysticism—James to Katz," *The Scottish Journal of Religious Studies* 3, no. 1 (Spring 1982): 3–14; Deirdre Green, "Unity in Diversity," *The Scottish Journal of Religious Studies* 3, no. 1 (Spring 1982): 46–58.
97. Jürgen Habermas, *Strukturwandel der Öffentlichkeit.*
98. See Harold Laski, *Studies in the Problem of Sovereignty* (New Haven: Yale University Press, 1917), 211–38.
99. Op.cit., 202.
100. See David Nicholls, *The Pluralist State* (New York: St. Martin's Press, 1975), 39.
101. John Henry Cardinal Newman, *Certain Difficulties Felt by Anglicans in Catholic Teaching* (London: Longmans Green, 1900), 2:243.
102. Op.cit., 2: 261.
103. "The Critical Function of the Concept of the Church in Nineteenth-Century Theology," in Charles Davis and others, *Community and Critique in Nineteenth-Century Theology* (Montreal: Interuniversity Centre for European Studies, 1980), 7–22.
104. David Tracy, *The Analogical Imagination: Christian Theology and the Culture of Pluralism* (New York: Crossroad, 1981).
105. Alexander Dru, *The Church in the Nineteenth Century: Germany* 1800–1918 (London: Burns & Oates, 1963), 42.

106. Josef R. Geiselmann, "Kirche und Frömmigkeit in den geistigen Bewegungen der ersten Hälfte des 19 Jahrhunderts (J.M. Sailer)," in J. Danielou and Herbert Vorgrimler, eds., *Sentire Ecclesiam: Das Bewusstsein von der Kircke als gestaltende Kraft der Frömmigkeit* (Freiburg: Herder, 1961), 475.
107. Ibid., 485–86.
108. Ibid., 506.
109. Ernst Troeltsch, *The Social Teaching of the Christian Churches* (London: Allen & Unwin, 1931), 2: 1008–09.
110. Ernst Troeltsch, "Schleiermacher und die Kirche," in *Schleiermacher der Philosoph des Glaubens,* Moderne Philosophie no. 6. (Berlin-Schöneberg: Buchverlag der "Hilfe," 1910), 9–35.
111. See Charles Davis, "The Theological Career of Historical Criticism of the Bible," *Cross Currents* 32, no. 3 (Fall 1982): 267–84.
112. David Kelsey, *The Uses of Scripture in Recent Theology* (Philadelphia: Fortress Press, 1975).
113. George A. Lindbeck, *The Nature of Doctrine: Religion and Theology in a Postliberal Age* (Philadelphia: Westminster Press, 1984).
114. *A Second Collection: Papers by Bernard J.F. Lonergan,* 258–59.
115. Hans W. Frei, *The Eclipse of Biblical Narrative: A Study in Eighteenth and Nineteenth Century Hermeneutics* (New Haven and London: Yale University Press, 1974). See my own development of the theme in "The Theological Career of Historical Criticism of the Bible," *Cross Currents* 32, no. 3 (Fall 1982), especially 278–79.
116. I have taken the point from an unpublished paper of Hans Frei, thought I have elaborated it in my own way.
117. Tom Bottomore, "Sociology," in David McLellan, ed., *Marx: the First Hundred Years* (Fontana Paperbacks, 1983), 117.
118. I am echoing some remarks of Leszek Kolakowski about Marxism-Leninism in "The Legacy of Marx: An Interview with Leszek Kolakowski," *The Tablet,* 12 March 1983, 232.
119. David Tracy, *The Analogical Imagination,* 100–03.
120. Richard Rorty, *Philosophy and the Mirror of Nature,* 389.
121. Wilfred Cantwell Smith, *Towards a World Theology,* 193.
122. For an analysis and critique of Habermas, see my *Theology and Political Society* (Cambridge: 1980), *passim.*

Index